THE STEP BY STEP GUIDE TO
FLOWER ARRANGING

THE STEP BY STEP GUIDE TO
FLOWER ARRANGING

the
apple
press

ACKNOWLEDGEMENTS

My loving and grateful thanks to my family and friends without whose help this book would have been impossible to prepare.

Many thanks to the Reverend Raymond Martin of St. John's Pauntley (Dick Whittington's church), who wrote the notes on the significance of the Paschal Candle; to Dr. Hermann Bomeke of Friesdorf Horticultural College, Germany, who provided pictures of Advent and Christmas designs, and to members of the Korean International Floral Art Association for the pictures they supplied.

Thanks to the publisher who is sufficiently interested in the subject of flower arranging to publish the book and, it goes without saying, many thanks to the flower enthusiasts all over the world who read it.

There can never be 'famous last words' written about such an evergreen and absorbing subject as flower arranging, but it is hoped, of course, that more and more people will be inspired by our world of flowers.

A QUINTET BOOK

Published by Apple Press Ltd
Unit 3, Ashville Trading Estate,
Royston Rd, Baldock, Herts SG7

Reprinted 1987

Reprinted 1988

ISBN 1 85076 019 5

This book was designed and produced by
Quintet Publishing Limited
6 Blundell Street, London N7 9BH

Designer Michael Orton
Editor Dorothea Hall
Editorial assistants Ray Martin, Fiona St. Aubyn
Photographer Ian Howes

Typeset in Great Britain by
Leaper and Gard Limited, Bristol
Colour Origination in Hong Kong by Universal
Colour Scanning Limited,
Hong Kong
Printed in Hong Kong by Leefung-Asco Printers
Limited

CONTENTS

Flower arranging is an art that anyone can master – and the lovely thing about it is that you can make as much or as little of it as you wish.

You may first have shown an interest in arranging flowers as a child when you used a jam jar from the kitchen to hold a bunch of wild flowers picked from the hedgerows – bluebells, primroses, marsh marigolds – a delicate mixture of colours. And perhaps you were saddened when they wilted and died soon afterwards even in quite deep clear water.

But wild flowers (and others) will last in water if treated properly at the moment of picking. Always bear in mind that you are handling living material, that no two blooms are identical, and that flowers possess a dignity that should never be diminished.

Records indicate that flowers and herbs have been cultivated throughout history, not so much for decoration as for their medicinal properties. However, there are few records of any design techniques earlier than the nineteenth century except in China and Japan.

In the Victorian era printing techniques improved markedly so that many more books were available to the public. There was lively interest in the arts, science and horticulture. Botanists began to travel all over the world, bringing back many new species to enrich the existing indigenous flora.

In keeping with this gracious and expansive way of life, flowers and plants were used to embellish homes and gardens; estate gardeners indulged in an exciting new art form which involved growing and arranging flowers, fruit and exotic plants for special occasions.

Happily now, in the twentieth century, flower arranging is available for everyone's pleasure. This book does not set out to lay down rules and regulations – too many of these can stifle creativity and individuality. Rather, it sets out to guide, to suggest ways of bringing pleasure to oneself and others, and embellishing your home by bringing inside a small segment of nature to provide an ever-changing environment of colour, form and perfume.

Arranging flowers, no matter when or where, will reward you with a lifetime of delight.

Ronald M. Coleman

CHAPTER ONE

EQUIPMENT AND TECHNIQUES

A few simple tools are all that one needs to begin
flower arranging. The more specialized items can be added
as you become more adventurous in your design.
Flower arranging need not involve a large investment –
containers, for instance, can usually be found in most homes in
all shapes and sizes. A good pair of flower scissors and secateurs,
a sharp knife, watering can and floral foam are some of the basic
implements discussed in the chapter and are recommended as
valuable aids to technique.

BASIC EQUIPMENT

A selection of the correct tools and equipment can help tremendously in flower arranging to build up confidence and prevent frustration. If you start your collection with one or two basic pieces and add others as and when they are needed, or as your skills progress, the initial cost will not be too great. Choose well-designed equipment which should be easy and comfortable to use.

Scissors There are several very good makes now available in varying price ranges. If possible, try one or two for 'grip', and test the weight and balance in your hand. You may like a heavy tool – I prefer a light one. See if there is enough space for the fingers and thumb. Some of the so-called 'flower scissors' have very small rings which imprison your fingers. These are difficult to use and are therefore not recommended.

Shears with long-blades such as those used in the kitchen and by dressmakers, are also very handy for flower arrangers. They are ideal for cutting ribbon, fabric and fine wire. For the very heavy wire stems of some fabric flowers and foliage, you will need small secateurs, and for large woody branches, you will need gardening secateurs.

A sharp knife is an indispensable piece of equipment. It can be used for trimming all kinds of stems, and for pointing the tips so that they can be driven easily into foam. It can also be used for cutting floral foam and for removing thorns from rose stems. This need not cost a lot of money – my favourite is an inexpensive little knife which is light and well-balanced, and, when sheathed, fits conveniently into a pocket or handbag. Moreover it can be finely sharpened to make a really efficient tool.

Floral foam is available in several makes but you should experiment with the various options to find out which one suits your particular needs. There are two distinct types: the green one used for fresh arrangements and the pale brown, dry one used exclusively for dried and fabric flower designs. The brown foam is much more dense and solid and should never be soaked. Conversely, the green variety is not solid enough to hold stems firmly and should not be used dry.

Each type is available in several shapes and sizes. The large brick is made especially for large arrangements while cylinders and squares which are about one-third of a large block in size, are useful for most small or medium-sized designs. One can, of course, cut a large block to the required size, but this will produce a certain amount of unavoidable waste. As each brand of foam varies, it is almost impossible to say precisely how long it will take for a particular size to become saturated. If you are using it for the first time, the following guide will be useful. Put the foam into a bowl or bucket of water and let it sink to the bottom. Allow 30 minutes for small blocks and up to two hours, or longer, for large blocks. Floral foam is a fascinating substance. It is feather-light when dry and really heavy when it is completely saturated. Remember to cut this type of foam after it has been thoroughly soaked. To be certain it has taken in the maximum amount of water, cut right across the block and if the centre is still pale green, then it needs longer soaking.

Flower food is sold either in small packets in powder form or as a liquid essence which must be diluted according to the directions on the bottle. The packets contain enough powder to make about 2 pints of solution. As well as the nourishment, which will noticeably prolong the life of your flowers, the preparation also contains a germ inhibitor specially formulated to keep the water pure. In fact, the manufacturers of some brands advise you not to change the vase water claiming that even summer flowers, such as scabious, larkspur and sweet william, which are renowned for polluting the water, will keep fresh in the solution. Use it for conditioning your flowers before arranging them and also for saturating the foam.

Receptacles It is advisable to keep a few plastic saucers handy which are useful for arranging designs in containers that will not hold water, such as baskets. However, since they have absolutely no decorative appeal, they should be regarded only as receptacles and not containers. They are available in varying sizes, in green, white or black.

Oasis-fix is a dark green, malleable substance similar in texture to Plasticine, a modelling clay. It has a toffee-like appearance which never sets completely hard, but will stick almost any dry surfaces together. It is used extensively for attaching wired flowers to their bases, for securing a receptacle inside another container, and also for fixing candle-cups to vases or candle-sticks. It does not however, adhere safely to glass or highly-glazed surfaces. As Oasis-fix is oil-based, it should not be applied directly to special wood surfaces such as wooden trays, table tops or fruit bowls for example. To prevent these surfaces from becoming stained, first apply a piece of adhesive tape or narrow masking tape, before putting a small amount of fixative on top.

It is a very useful substance for the majority of flower-arranging techniques. It can be bought by the roll and as it is used only in small amounts, a roll may last a very long time and fortunately, does not deteriorate with keeping.

Prongs are made from pale green plastic and have four long pins on to which a block of foam is impaled for greater stability. They are inexpensive and cost very little to buy, and may be attached to the container with Oasis-fix. Remember that the base of the prong and the container must be completely dry. Unless the container is needed for something else, the prong can be left in place after discarding the flowers when it will be ready for the next arrangement. The Oasis-fix will never dry brick-hard, but the longer

the prong is left attached, the firmer it becomes.

Clear adhesive tape may be used for securing the foam to the container, especially for heavy designs, or if the arrangement has to be moved by vehicle. Smaller designs will be sufficiently firm if the foam is simply impaled on a prong, but for gladioli, dahlias, chrysanthemums and in fact, all heavy and long-stemmed flowers, it is important to have the base really firmly anchored. Some flower arrangers use green or white Oasis-tape, but this is visible on the container, whereas clear adhesive tape will allow the colour of the container to show through. Both kinds of tape should be fixed to a completely dry surface.

A watering can is a very useful piece of equipment to have amongst your tools. It is quite indispensable for watering house plants, and also for adding water to flower arrangements when necessary. Even though you may previously have thoroughly soaked the foam and added water initially, there is bound to be some dehydration. As flowers should be taking in water all the time, it is essential that the foam is not allowed to dry out.

A spray is very handy for giving your arrangement a final spray with clear water – obviously when you have spent time and trouble making the design you want it to last as long as possible. In addition to providing water for the stems a daily spray with a mister helps to keep the materials really fresh, especially if the room is warm or during hot weather.

Well-designed equipment helps you to work confidently and calmly. This watering can (*left*) comfortably holds 3 pints (1.5l) of water. The handle is easy to grasp and the flange around the top of the can prevents water from spilling out. The spout is set low so that it does not have to be tipped steeply when watering.

EQUIPMENT AND TECHNIQUES

Basic equipment: 1 Well-designed watering can. **2** Packets of long-life powder for fresh flowers. **3** Oasis-fix, an oil-based fixative which can be removed from surfaces with white spirit. **4** Narrow-bladed knife sufficiently long to cut through soaked foam. **5** and **6** Stainless steel scissors and mini-secateurs, which are light, well-balanced and easy to handle. **7** Clear adhesive tape about ³⁄₈ in (10 mm) wide. **8** White vase. **9** Dry foam used for dried and fabric flower arrangements. **10** Large block of green foam — easily cut when soaked in water or a long-life solution. **11** Small cyclindrical shape of green foam — a convenient size for plastic saucers and small containers. **12** Plastic water spray and mister. **13** Small plastic saucer. **14** Prongs.

8

9

10

11

12

13

14

SPECIAL EQUIPMENT

The array of special equipment available should not be allowed to curb your enthusiasm for, above all, the flowers themselves are the most important factor in successful flower arranging. None of this equipment is essential to the success of a simple flower design and many arrangers may never use any of it. But as your flower arranging skills improve and your interests widen, there are one or two special pieces of equipment that you may find useful to have 'on the shelf'. It is better to acquire your equipment as you need it and not just because you think you ought to have it.

Ribbons can be an elegant addition to many flower arrangements and gifts so the more colours you have to choose from, the better. The polypropylene or paper ribbon in particular is excellent for decorating bouquets. It is totally water-resistant and can be torn into strips of the required width. Woven ribbon, as opposed to the paper variety, is available in a wide range of colours and widths and is quite water-tolerant.

Pinholders are available in several sizes. They are useful for anchoring Japanese-style designs, and also for securing heavy branches. The illustration shows a pinholder and container made in one piece, which is intended to be placed in or on another base. The gold-spray finish makes it considerably more elegant than a plastic saucer. It is also quite heavy and consequently very stable in use.

Candle-cups are available in gold, black or white. They are small containers specially shaped with a 'foot' that can be fitted into the neck of a bottle or candlestick, or it can be secured to the top of a narrow-necked container.

Colour sprays may be needed now and again to complement a special colour scheme, such as gold, silver and bronze around Christmas-time. Old containers can be quickly revitalized with spray paint and new ones can be 'antiqued' using a

Special Equipment: 1 Roll of water-resistant satin ribbon about 50 yds (47 m) long. **2** Polypropylene ribbon available in 100 yds (94 m) rolls. **3** A combined pinholder and small container. **4** Candle-cups. **5** and **6** Gold spray and colour spray. When using, it is advisable to wear plastic gloves for protection. **7** Clearlife. Two light coats are better than one generous coat. **8** One of several preparations for spraying onto green leaves to make them shine. **9** Floral tape used to cover wires and to seal the stem-end of support wires. **10** Stub wires, which can be bought in a variety of sizes and thicknesses. **11** Fine silver binding wire.

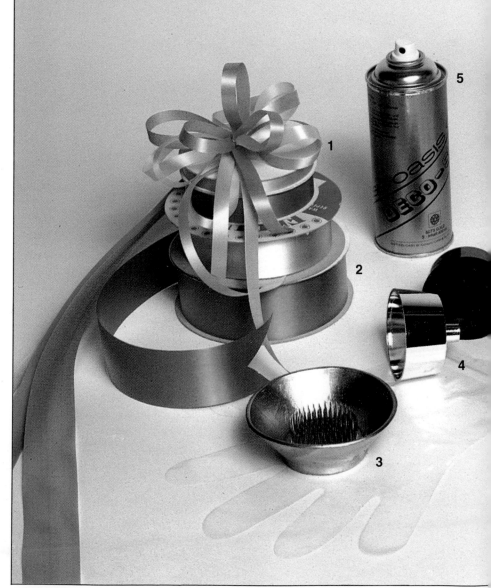

combination of sprays.

Proprietary brand sprays can also be applied to living flowers and foliage, wood, plastic and even candles – to change or enhance their original colours. The sprays, however, should be used on living material with very great care and treated as an expedient rather than a general practice.

Clearlife is a colourless spray which helps to prolong the vase life of some fresh flowers. It prevents them from shattering, and flowers such as larkspur, delphinium, cornflower and eremurus, indeed, any that drop their petals, can be 'held' a little longer with a light spray when the arrangement is completed.

Stub wires are useful for supporting flowers whose stems might become curved as they take up water. *Note*: a wire support should never be used to revitalize a fading flower but rather to control a fresh one. If support is necessary, try to insert the wire either up or down through the centre of the stem. In this way, it will not be visible, and neither will the stem nor the petal formation be punctured, which would cause the material to dehydrate more rapidly.

Fine silver binding wire is used for fashioning ribbon bows, similar to the one illustrated. Make one loop and secure with a twist of silver wire. Make another loop securing it in the same place with the same length of wire. Continue adding loops until the bow is sufficiently full.

A less elaborate bow is made by folding the ribbon into a figure of eight and securing it across the centre with a taped wire. The floral tape will prevent the wire from rusting on to the ribbon, should it get wet, it also helps the wire to 'bite'.

Floral tape is used to cover non-silver wires. There are several varieties obtainable and one should experiment before deciding on any particular brand. It has been known to vary in performance in extreme climates.

CONDITIONING TECHNIQUES

Your material will presumably come from either the florist's shop, or the garden, or both. In either case, it will need a certain amount of care and attention before being arranged. This is called conditioning.

Garden flowers can be cut in the early morning or late evening. The moment a stem is severed from the parent plant, its life support is cut off. In order that the flower or foliage can continue to survive we compensate by putting it in water, preferably in a flower food solution. Not even this can give it all the nourishment it was getting from the root system, but it will help to prolong its freshness.

To condition our garden material, before cutting prepare a container of water, adding the correct amount of flower food. A deep plastic bucket is the most useful but it need not be completely filled. It has recently been established that most flowers do not, in effect, require deep water, the ideal depth being about 7 in (20 cm). Bulb-grown flowers are an exception and need only 3-4 in (8-10 cm). As you cut the flowers, strip off any leaves low down on the stems. Always carry them head downwards as this helps to retain any moisture in the stems. Before standing the material in water, use a very sharp knife and trim each stem end to a sharp point. The exposed angle will offer a larger surface to the water than if the stem were cut straight across.

Cutting the stem at the conditioning stage. Stems of garden flowers should be cut at a sharp angle and with a sharp knife before being stood in water.

Any stems carrying thorns, such as roses and some shrubs, should be trimmed, not only for easy handling while you are arranging, but to prevent the thorns from hooking into other flowers. To de-thorn roses, hold your knife blade almost flat against the stem and 'chop' each thorn away. Alternatively, the thorns can be pulled off one by one between finger and thumb but this is a very slow process. Garden roses rarely refuse to take up water. Amongst flowers which may need special attention are lilac, poppies, zinnias and marigolds. Lilac will take up water more readily if most of the foliage is stripped off. It also has very woody stems and prefers to be conditioned in hot water.

Poppies are supposedly very short-lived, but if the stems are instantly plunged into very hot water, or the end is sealed over a flame, they will last for several days. Their decorative quality is outstanding so special care is well worth the trouble.

Zinnias and large marigolds sometimes droop their heads just below the flower. The stems are hollow and seem incapable of supporting such magnificent flowers. Insert a wire inside the stem until it reaches the flower-head – this will keep it upright and the flower will take up water happily.

Draughts are, apart from the shortage of water, a flower's enemy, so set your material in a cool, draught-free place to rehabilitate before being arranged. Flowers do not really thrive in direct sunlight, particularly where the heat is concentrated through glass. But it is surprising how tolerant they are once they have been properly conditioned.

An appealing, well-balanced design should ideally include both buds and open flowers. However, a fully matured flower does not have as long a vase life as a younger bud or flower. This should be taken into consideration when planning the arrangement. So often the largest flower is set into the heart of a design, and when it fades the arrangement looks empty and disappointing.

Bulb-grown flowers are wonderfully trouble-free, though if they are cut *too* young, that is, if the bud is just too tight, the flower will never develop to its full beauty.

1 To condition and de-thorn roses, take a sharp knife and cut off any leaves which are growing on the lower part of the stem. Remember to work with the knife blade pointing away from the body.

2 With the blade of your knife almost flat against the stem, carefully remove the thorns at the base of the stem to give about a 5 in (13 cm) length of stem to hold.

3 With the knife blade at the same angle, and facing away from you, slice the remaining thorns off, finishing at the head.

Two pieces of gypsophila cut from the same branch being treated with a fixative spray (*above*). One of these stems was then placed in a flower food solution, the other in plain water. The benefit gained from the flower food treatment can be seen in the second photograph (*right*) taken a week later.

Flowers should never be cut in full sunshine. The best time is early morning or after sundown.

Material from the flower shop will already have been conditioned but the stems will callous over in transit and should therefore be re-cut. They can then be treated as flowers from the garden although they will not need to stay as long in the conditioning bucket before being arranged.

Most shop flowers will have been several hours, indeed even a few days, in transit during which time they have been without water. However, good conditioning will usually 'set them on their feet again', although some flowers, such as roses, occasionally refuse to take up water. In this case, re-cut the stem and stand the rose in hot water. This will soften the stem tissues and the flower will probably take up water within a few moments. Or, stand it in a carbonated liquid such as fizzy lemonade for example. The 'fizz' will drive the liquid up the stem while the sugar content feeds the flower.

Total immersion is used for most broad leaves. They respond well to being literally 'drowned' for several hours, after which they will last well for many days in the design. Hosta, caladium, dieffenbachia, wild arum, begonia rex, geranium and numerous other flowers benefit from this apparently drastic treatment. Roses that refuse to drink usually revive if totally submerged for several hours.

Heavy wooded stems such as chrysanthemums, branches of trees, flowering trees and shrubs should, if possible, be broken at the stem end with your fingers. If the branch is too tough to break this way, cut it with secateurs and condition in very hot water.

The concept of hammering hardwood stems to pulverize the end has been rejected on the basis that the 'fringed' stem that results is an ideal breeding ground for bacteria.

While on the subject of bacteria, it is worth pointing out that diseased materials should never be used and that all the containers you use for either conditioning or arranging should be kept perfectly clean. From time to time, they should be sterilized and cleaned thoroughly. Similarly your tools will also need to be cleaned. The blades of knives and scissors should be polished with steel wool and regularly sharpened.

CONTAINERS

From the beginning of time, containers must have been some of the first domestic 'implements'. For, apart from weapons, people had to have receptacles in which to carry and store liquid for drinking and, presumably for washing. And what is amazing is that now in the twentieth century, the basic shape is much the same as it was in the days before the Greek and Roman Empires.

To see a contemporary consignment of water and oil jars being unloaded on a busy Greek quayside is to be temporarily transported hundreds of years back in time. How logical in shape these traditional containers are. They are narrow at the neck to prevent evaporation, and at the same time, they are elegantly bulbous (if that is not a contradiction in terms), so that they hold a maximum amount of liquid. Bernard Leach, the father of handmade pottery in England, adopted the classic Greek container as the basis for so many of his designs, which have been copied by his students all over the world.

Flowers have been incorporated into ceremonial occasions in many countries through history. They have also been woven into garlands to grace banquets, used at funerals, and for greeting victorious military leaders on their return. Single flowers in quantity were scattered on the floors of rich citizens' homes as much for their perfume as for their beauty. If flowers were carried, they were usually fashioned into small nosegays, often with the idea of keeping other, less-attractive odours at bay. Hence the word 'nosegay'

Formal arrangements were usually contrived with flowering plants set into large containers. Many of these containers were extremely beautiful and we are fortunate that examples have been preserved in mosaics, paintings and tapestries, in stately homes and museums in many countries. It seems as though these objects were designed purely as art forms. Indeed, many of them are so beautiful in their own right that they were never intended to hold flowers – perhaps one shapely branch or a perfect stem of flowers for some very special occasion.

Until the early nineteenth century, few cut flowers were used in private homes. It was the fashion among the rich to decorate their homes with pictures of flowers, but of course the ordinary people could not afford pictures and so resorted to the real thing. Vases and containers, though not as ornate as those previously mentioned, were still strictly formal. They were deep, so as to hold plenty of water, and wide, which usually resulted in the arrangement either looking sparse or requiring a huge amount of material to fill it. Certain receptacles in the household were regarded as 'flower vases' and as far as we know, no other vessels were pressed into service.

This situation prevailed almost to the end of the nineteenth century, when interior decoration was at its most opulent. But after the First World War, certain values were dramatically changed. Furnishings became more streamlined, due

in no small measure to the lack of domestic help. For many people, this was real liberation – no longer did they have to live with heavy and overbearing 'heirlooms' cluttering small crowded living rooms. Interiors became noticeably less fussy: fabrics were plainer and colours less confused.

Fabrics, wallpaper, furniture and flower vases were produced with a simple handmade style – even then, many of these vases were still too large. Incidentally, the Japanese are expert in designing suitable bases and containers, and some of their smaller ones, with very narrow necks, are perfect for a single flower.

Along with this change in attitude to interior decoration was the upsurge of horticultural interest. However, until the early 1940s containers, certainly in Britain and America, were still somewhat stylized. Other countries led the way, not-

Choosing a Vase: A wide range of vases, in different shapes, sizes and colours, will help to bring variety and interest to your designs. Glass, porcelain, pottery and plastic containers (*left and below*) can all be used effectively.

Do not be afraid of patterned containers such as the porcelain jug below — with care, and thought they can enhance a floral design rather than clash with it.

If unglazed pots are used, a saucer or other suitable receptacle should be placed underneath to protect surfaces from water seepage.

ably Germany, Italy, and Japan, with new handmade designs created especially for those people newly interested in flower arranging. Now, many smaller, more logical containers are being produced in great quantities and flower arrangers have a tremendous choice.

Many people have now become more conscious of the innate possibilities of all types of containers, whether they have been specially designed for flowers or not. Indeed, this produces an added challenge since antique shops and the corner 'junk shop' can produce some real treasures in terms of size, shape, finish and general design.

It should be remembered that a collection of vases and containers does not come together overnight, and neither is it a good idea to buy too many at one time. They should be collected exactly as one might collect any other *objets d'art*: slowly and objectively, keeping your eye on local jumble sales and white elephant stalls where you may discover a real beauty. First of all, take a look at the receptacles you already have. Most homes have a selection of bowls, ornamental jars, perhaps a decanter without a stopper, or other silver, brass, wood, glass or pottery containers. Any type of material is suitable providing it is compatible with the flowers. Before you put a container or base into use, do check that it is watertight. If not, do not discard it. It is often quite easy to find a receptacle that does retain water to fit neatly inside. This might be a simple plastic container. Incidentally, the inside of every receptacle should be perfectly clean, as dirt and germs will noticeably shorten the vase life of your arrangement. Many containers can be filled with a strong bleach solution which will do all the work for you.

A container that is interesting in its own right, but far too strong a design for the delicate tolmiea and lily-of-the-valley. The undulating edge and sharp white of the vase's pattern conflict with the gentle curves and softer colouring of the flowers. This shape also poses the problem of masking the foam base.

A sad little collection of flowers (*above*) sunk deep in an awkward shaped container. *Below*: Anemones will arrange themselves quite well, but to expect them to do this in a coffee jar is a little optimistic. *Right*: This vase's narrow neck holds the anemones in a satisfying position.

CHAPTER TWO

BASIC
PRINCIPLES

Once you have learned the basic principles of
flower arranging you will be better able to express your own
individual flair and style. But – as with most things – it is
important first to learn the fundamental guidelines.
The information given in the chapter starts by describing
how to anchor your material firmly to a base before you begin
a design. It explains the four geometric forms – horizontal,
vertical, symmetrical and asymmetrical – on which most
arrangements are based, and it describes how to use balance,
proportion, texture and contrast to make a successful and
pleasing arrangement.

HOLDING AND FIXING FLOWERS

A successful flower arrangement depends on how firmly it is anchored to the base. There are several methods of preparing containers and bases: floral foam is now so much a part of the flower arranger's basic equipment that it is difficult to remember how we ever made an arrangement without it. But, efficient though it is, it is certainly not the only way of supporting the material: in fact, some flowers prefer to be directly in water whenever possible. Proteas, in particular, last far longer if they can stand in deep water, while gladioli, although they last quite well when arranged in foam, really prefer to have their stems in water.

Wire mesh, pinholders, moss, sand and cut branches all help to support the material and your choice of method must be dictated by the size and type of design, as well as the material being used.

Many arrangers like to use mesh as well as foam. This is a very valid method, particularly for rather large heavy material. Mesh used alone should be crumpled to fit the shape of the container, preferably with some left well above the rim. If you press it in too low, you will have no support for your lateral stems. Even though it may seem fairly firm, it is advisable to secure it to the rim of the container with adhesive tape or string.

If you are using a container with an extremely high glaze, or made of glass, the

Soaked floral foam will need to be secured to a shallow 'open' base. (*Above and top*: It can be impaled on prongs which have been attached to a plastic saucer by Oasis-fix. Both prongs and container must be clean and dry if the Oasis-fix is to adhere firmly.)

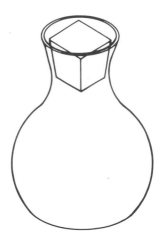

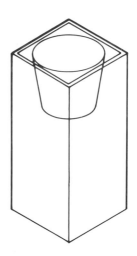

An old-fashioned wire support in a wide-mouthed urn. Both support and urn pose problems: the urn requires a very large number of flowers for a balanced design, and the wire support (superseded by more modern floral foam and mesh) is very difficult to handle. Definitely a container to leave well alone.

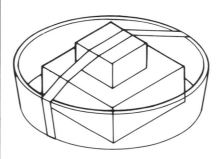

A foam base should stand at least 1in (2 cm) above the rim of your container. Deep bowls may need two pieces of foam stacked to achieve sufficient height. A second smaller piece may be impaled on the first and the two secured firmly to the container with adhesive tape.

It is important to cut soaked foam to a size that will fit securely into the neck of your container. A square piece should be wedged into a round neck and a round piece into a square neck. This ensures a good fit and leaves room for adding more water when necessary.

A large pot of this kind (*right*) and also in the diagram (*far right*) can be made smaller by inserting a smaller pot into its neck. This solves the problem of securing the foam sufficiently well to carry a big design. It also reduces the amount of water — and therefore of additional weight — needed to keep the flowers and foliage fresh.

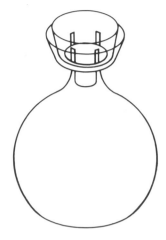

In large containers with narrow necks, candle cups may be inserted to reduce the size, but even the largest cup may be unable to carry sufficient foam for a big design.

Mesh is particularly useful as extra support for heavy designs. It should be fixed to your container with a loop of adhesive tape secured on either side. With a large container, the mesh may need to be secured in three places.

Oasis-fix will not adhere firmly enough. The solution is to fold a piece of tissue or paper kitchen towel and use it as a small non-skid mat for the foam. The block should then be fixed firmly with sellotape.

Sand is sometimes used at the base of a container for dried flowers. But be very careful, for sand is heavy and if too much is used, it could make the base of the vase fall out.

If you are totally without any support mechanism, cut some stems or small branches to the depth of the vase. Almost fill the aperture and they will give the necessary support, though a design with spreading lateral lines would not be practical.

In deciding the size of foam, the main thing to remember is that once you have inserted a stem you have made a hole which obviously weakens the block. If you have never used foam, cut a piece you feel will take every stem comfortably. If your container has a round opening, then choose a square piece of foam, and vice versa. This allows for a better fit and there will be a space left to insert the spout of the watering can for adding more water.

The depth of the foam is easier to estimate. Since most arrangements have some lateral stems, make sure the foam stands at last 1 in (2 cm) above the rim of the container otherwise you will be trying to insert stems into mid-air.

Pinholders of varying sizes are useful for shallow containers. They are very heavy and need no fixative to hold them in position. They can also be used together with wire mesh for larger arrangements that include heavy branches and flowers with large stems, for example, arum lilies. They will also tolerate foam, but much prefer to be directly in water.

Large containers, of course, present a greater challenge than smaller ones. For example, the type of brass container sometimes used in churches becomes impossibly heavy if filled with water, while the neck is often rather small. One solution to the problem is to locate a smaller container that will effectively slot into the neck thus forming a kind of inner lining. Alternatively, a large candle-cup may be used, though even the largest size may not be big enough to hold a piece of foam large enough to support a really large design.

Each time you make an arrangement, try to keep the size of foam used down to a minimum. Although it is far easier to design into a large block, it needs a lot of material to mask it which is, at least, time-consuming. But never make it so small as to risk the foam collapsing. Like many other skills, there are certain guidelines to follow, but eventually, one becomes experienced in what your tools – in this case, the foam – can do for you.

Remember, before you begin a design, to add water to the container as soon as you are satisfied that the base is firm. It is far easier at this stage than when all the material is in place.

In order to travel with a design, it is safer to pour the water out when the arrangement is finished, and take a small can with you to refill the container once it is in place. The well-soaked foam will keep the flowers fresh for many hours but in a warm atmosphere you will get a longer vase life from the flowers if the container is kept filled with water.

1 Oasis-fix will not adhere well to a highly-glazed surface. A damp tissue placed in the base of this shallow compote will stop floral foam from sliding.

2 The foam, resting on the paper, is fixed with sellotape. The two pieces of stem seen here will prevent the tape from biting into the foam.

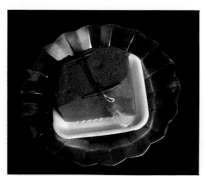

3 Here soaked foam has been laid on a polystyrene tray to protect the surface of the silver container. The foam is firmly secured to the tray with sellotape.

4 For display purposes, a damaged leaf can be patched on the underside with a section from another leaf. Use a little glue, plus a little care, to complete the disguise.

For this contemporary free-style arrangement (*left*) a large pinholder is sufficiently heavy to sit firmly in the shallow highly-glazed dish. The decorative stones help to mask the pinholder so that the minimum of foliage is needed. Each stem should be held very close to the pinholder and impaled firmly (*above*).

THE FOUR BASIC FORMS

Each of the four basic forms described here provides a simple geometric structure on which a flower arrangement can be built. The materials you have at hand and where you decide to place your arrangement, will determine the form you choose to work from.

The history of flower arranging dates back to ancient times and all kinds of patterns and forms have evolved through the ages, mainly under the influence of the West and the Far East. The Japanese, for example, have practised the art for well over a thousand years, and they are renowned for their pure classic asymmetrical designs. Books, paintings and mosaics are a valuable historic record – there are the Byzantine floral mosaics in Ravenna with their tall symmetrical designs, the stylized Dutch and Flemish flower paintings of the seventeenth and eighteeneth centuries, and the proliferation of books and magazines on the art of flower arranging in Victorian times. Definite rules of arrangement, however, were established during this century.

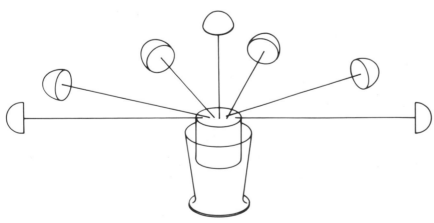

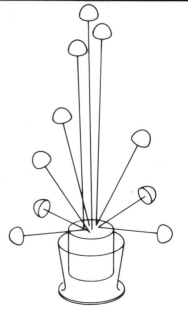

Horizontal arrangement (*above*) of pink carnations, pink bud tulips and gypsophila. One more tulip is needed on the left to complete the symmetrical form.

Vertical design (*top right*) of tall blue iris and yellow double gerbera. To keep their upright form, the gerberas are supported with an inner wire. The method of wiring is explained on page 33.

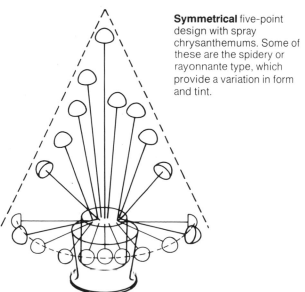

Symmetrical five-point design with spray chrysanthemums. Some of these are the spidery or rayonnante type, which provide a variation in form and tint.

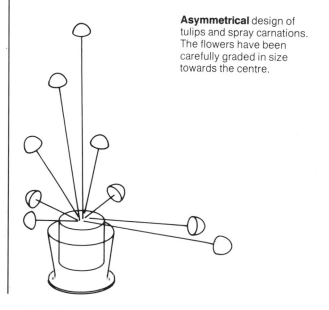

Asymmetrical design of tulips and spray carnations. The flowers have been carefully graded in size towards the centre.

HORIZONTAL ARRANGEMENTS

Arrangements with a horizontal emphasis are particularly suitable for table centrepieces where the design should not be so high and bushy that it acts as a hedge between the diners. It is also an excellent style for 'window-dressing' an empty fireplace in summer, or a mantelshelf, particularly in a fairly small room where a tall design might otherwise be overpowering.

While too many rigid rules and regulations applied to what is not only a technical skill but also an art form, can be stultifying to progress, some of the most obvious rules do make sense. For example, most basket shapes would suggest a horizontal arrangement and that the handle should be left free from encompassing foliage so that it is easy to hold. On the other hand, there may be instances where the designer might feel it necessary to place a few tall flowers above the handle. However, in order to break the rules, one must first learn to apply them. To avoid frustration and disappointment, it is better to stick to basics until you feel your designing is becoming more fluid.

Sometimes a flower arranger is invited to place flowers on the church altar, though in some churches this is not

A subtle horizontal design from Korea, composed of pink dahlias, yellow roses and white antirrhinums enlivened with variegated foliage.

allowed. A horizontal design is usually the most suitable and should be kept symmetrical to balance the existing symmetry, and often the simplicity, of other appointments nearby. Having completed the design, always go to the back of the church to check that the central flower is not taller than the cross, which is either on or just behind the altar. It is usual when making a horizontal arrangement to establish the spread of the design first. Fix these two lines first and then decide the height and the depth and work within this framework.

Arrangements for the dining table whether at home or at a banquet are

Carnations, with a frosting of gypsophila. The tulips were added last to give variation of colour, shape and texture.

usually horizontal otherwise no one would be able to see or be seen. The maximum width of such designs is crucial, for there must be ample space for the guests to eat or, in the case of a banquet, speakers' notes and microphones. Graceful and near-symmetrical horizontal designs, sometimes joined with ribbons or ropes of green foliage can effectively enhance what might otherwise be a rather stark dining table. This is one of the many occasions that offers both scope and challenge to any designing enthusiast.

1 To make a horizontal design, first decide on the colour and texture of your design and gather your materials together. Here the yellow and orange of the flowers pick up the colouring of the foliage at the centre.

2 Cut well-soaked floral foam so that it fits the container you have chosen.

3 Not every design need be constructed from the outside inwards. Begin in the middle of this design, masking the foam with foliage and roughly describing the shape intended.

4 Now insert your line flowers.

5 Strengthen the lines with the addition of more flowers, being careful not to overcrowd the arrangement.

VERTICAL ARRANGEMENTS

A simple description of vertical is that the line is at right angles to the horizon. If one then translates horizon into container-rim, it will give a good idea of how material should be set in place. However, most things turn out better if a plan of action is followed and a flower arrangement ought, in effect, to begin with a plan, based on a logical framework.

First establish whether the arrangement is to be a facing design – that is, viewed from the front only – or an all-round design. This affects the position of the first main stem. For a facing design, the main line must be set in towards the back of the foam, and for an all-round arrangement, it should be set in the centre of the foam.

The main line should be straight and definitive, and establish the maximum height of the arrangement. Then, two or three more lines should be inserted very close to the first one and parallel to it, each one slightly shorter than the previous one. These will emphasize the main line and help to make it visually stronger.

The next decision is to determine the maximum width of the design. For a facing arrangement, insert two lateral stems aiming towards the position where the main line was inserted.

For an all-round design, insert five stems of equal length radiating from the central line.

All that remains to be done is to add further material at intervals, keeping within your established framework. Take care not to crowd the material – it is always better to have too little rather than too much.

Strong vertical arrangements of purple irises softened by downward curving stems of yellow forsythia (*right*) and a charming combination of freesias with chrysanthemums (*far right*). Notice the interesting positions of the flower heads and the way in which profile and full views combine to make a flowering composition.

Straight-stemmed flowers like the gerbera (*above*) are particularly suited to vertical designs. The gerbera may curve, but wiring will ensure that the flower remains upright.

1 To wire a flower, insert a piece of wire of the correct thickness downwards through the centre of the flower stem into the middle of the flower head.

2 Press the wire gently but firmly back into the centre of the flower with the blade of your knife. Care is needed to ensure the flower remains undamaged.

SYMMETRICAL
ARRANGEMENTS

This is the purest form of all design. Perfect symmetry or visual balance is present in classical architecture, sculpture, tapestries, medieval paintings and containers, yet few of us are consciously aware of it. Even the word itself suggests grace and elegance.

The technical definition however, is far more mundane meaning that the object should be divided into two parts, both being equal in content. Translated into terms of flower arranging, this does not mean that all designs have to be facing. They can be circular, oval, horizontal or vertical, as long as they can be equally divided. Thus, a design with vertical emphasis may also be symmetrical, or the reverse, for it might quite possibly be asymmetrical and still be vertical.

As few flowers are identical, it is not easy to achieve perfect symmetry with living material. Therefore, an arranger is not expected to measure the two sections exactly for height, width and depth. Your design should rather appear to be symmetrical, giving a satisfying visual balance, bearing in mind, of course, that the basic disciplines should be respected. If your lines are well-placed and the materials carefully chosen, then successful results should follow. A simple arrangement can be made by placing an even number of stems at either side of the central stem.

In choosing the material it is probably easier to get a satisfactory result if you use not more than three types of flower, that is, flowers of differing shapes and sizes, such as delphiniums, roses and spray chrysanthemums. Apart from the type of flower and colour, the classic 'recipe' includes *line* flowers, which are the materials that give gradation, normally with buds and semi-open flowers, plus materials for *emphasis*. These are usually mature blooms, often of a strong, clear colour and shape.

Strong, clear lines are first established (*inset*) for this beautiful symmetrical arrangement of yellow double freesias, darker yellow spray chrysanthemums and purple liatris, with interesting dark green foliage, to emphasize the yellow blooms.

Your choice of colour will naturally play an important role in determining symmetry. You may, in fact, make a design which is entirely symmetrical from the point of view of line, yet if the colour values are off-balance, it will never appear to be symmetrical. Do not let this deter you from making symmetrical arrangements for table centrepieces and display. The style cannot possibly be mastered in one easy lesson, so keep trying out different types of materials during each season of the year. Remember that it is better to begin with a simple design and graduate to more complicated ones as you gain confidence.

For this arrangement the base is first masked with green hellebore (*above*) before the three main lines are set in place (*below*).

Notice (*right*) how the third flower down to the right of centre has been placed so as to avoid too formal an effect.

ASYMMETRICAL ARRANGEMENTS

This form of design is the reverse of the symmetrical type – which is, that each side should be different, possibly in content and certainly from the point of view of line and emphasis.

However, as with the other forms, it needs a firm framework on which to build. So, although the main line may not necessarily be set into the middle of the arrangement, it must be seen to be the main line that runs straight into the centre of the design.

Asymmetrical arrangements can also be set vertically or horizontally, but care should be taken so that they are not confused with free-style designs.

However, try not to become intimidated by too many definitions, rules and regulations. These few pointers are intended to help and not to confuse. When you are making an arrangement, imagine, in essence, that the framework is made up of bare twigs which you will then 'dress' with flowers and foliage. Keep the basic structure simple and well-defined to ensure a successful arrangement.

White jug and flowers in the first stages of preparation (*above*). Foam is wedged into the neck and the main lines are set in place. Notice the small but very definite bud carnations describing the structure.

At the next stage (*above*), existing lines are strengthened with more flowers, and some foliage is inserted. The main lines are now to some extent masked.

Vertical emphasis. Tulips and spray carnations in an elegant vase.

Pink carnations alone would be rather bland, so a little red alstroemeria is added. Notice how the main structure is kept, while at the same time flowers and foliage is added.

A strong structure described with lemon antirrhinums (*left*), which is repeated at varying lengths. Brown spray chrysanthemums at the heart of the design provide variation in colour and form. *Above*: A mixed arrangement of freesia, spiced with a few stems of tolmiea and strengthened at the heart with alchemilla foliage.

BALANCE AND PROPORTION

In flower arranging both balance and proportion, like colour values, are largely a matter for the individual eye. However, one cannot escape the fact that *actual* balance is needed for the design to be stable. It will either balance or fall over – it is as simple as that. It may seem impossible for arrangements to collapse and overbalance, but they do, with very disappointing results. Fortunately there are several technical ways of preventing this.

It may clarify the situation to pinpoint one or two problem areas. The first one is the size of the foam block. The size needed is most difficult to resolve since everyone works differently. But before cutting your foam, decide what kind of material you plan to use. If it includes heavy woody stems, or thick stemmed flowers such as gladioli and delphiniums for example, or heavy blooms such as chrysanthemums and dahlias, then you will need a fairly large and deep piece of foam. It should be remembered that every time a stem is driven into a block of foam, it makes a hole exactly the size of the stem. So, if you begin without a clear plan and have to change the position of the stems many times, the block is weakened still further.

In most cases, you may use only one or two chunky stems with quite delicate flowers such as spray carnations, candytuft and other lightweight annuals, or even spray chrysanthemums.

In deciding the depth of the foam, you will soon see, with a little experience, when a deeper block is required. For instance, a horizontal arrangement will need more than a vertical design.

When all the foregoing points have been sorted out in your own mind, and really, it only takes a moment or two, your next step is to make absolutely sure that the foam block is going to remain firm in its seating. Where practical, use an Oasis-prong plus adhesive tape wrapped around at least twice. When it comes to tackling the design, it is a good idea, if you are not too sure of your plan, to 'sketch' the lines out on the table with some of the

1 To make a two-tier arrangement First, choose two basketware trays. Loop strong wire off-centre through the larger, bottom one and twist this over a soaked foam block, using small pieces of foliage to protect the edges.

2 Pull the two ends of wire up through the top tray, which will now rest on the foam below, held in place by the wire. Flatten the wire ends.

3 Take a small tin lid and attach it to the top basket tray with Oasis-fix, again off-centre, and fill it with a piece of soaked floral foam.

4 Begin the design by placing the four stems of allium. Insert one stem laterally into the bottom foam block and the others into the top tier block.

5 Insert the foliage into the foam on each level and add the carnation stems and the remaining green material.

6 The completed design (*opposite*), fully exploiting the quality of the allium.

An unimaginative use of four allium (*above*).
They clearly want a little support material,
and the stark stems need some back up.
Adding deep red spray carnations and
foliage in a design on two levels makes a far
more interesting and dramatic use of the
allium.

material. Or, you could even work into an old piece of foam as a practice run.

The pedestal is probably the type of design that gives the most difficulty where actual balance is concerned. This is discussed in connection with church designs elsewhere in the book, but at the risk of being repetitive, begin by placing your material right at the back of the foam. To make it safe, put your point of balance two-thirds towards the back of the foam inserting only a few stems into the front portion.

Visual balance is affected or influenced as much by the colour, size, shape and texture of the material, as the way in which it is used.

One of the best critics of any arrangement is a camera lens, for one's eye can see what one intends it to see, which is not always what is recorded by the camera. So, whenever possible, take pictures of your designs, aiming the lens exactly at the centre of the arrangement. It is not fair on yourself to shoot from either too high or too low for then the result will appear to be off-balance.

This pottery container (*above*) is too deep and too wide for such delicate flowers as sweet-scented freesias. The rough texture of the pot is also too heavy and tends to overpower the flowers.

Right: A solid-looking handmade pot is well suited to these large gerbera, arresting in shape, texture and colour. The pot was prepared with a good-sized block of soaked foam, wedged into its neck and further secured with adhesive tape.

Another way of checking your final design is to leave it, if possible, for 24 hours and then look at it as if seeing it for the first time when your judgement will be sharper.

Proportion should be seen in every aspect of the design, including the materials used, the proportion of the complete design in relation to the container, and the relationship of the chosen design with its environment.

While varying sizes of material can be used to create a good design, they should be selected with care so that they blend together. Thus, an arrangement of gerbera and freesia might be out of proportion. Even the *masking* and *support* foliage can sometimes upset good proportion. When using delicate flowers, such as freesias or Singapore orchids, the foliage should not be too large or heavy from the point of view of colour or texture. However, problems of bad proportion regarding the use of materials are, happily, few and far between. On the other hand, the choice of container is sometimes in error, for it may be too large or too small for the material. This fault is easily corrected by substituting another container.

A well-balanced arrangement of freesias in this chalice type vase (*above left*). But be warned — a wide-mouthed container like this demands many flowers if a satisfying design is to be achieved.

Above: This old-fashioned type of kitchen jar has become very popular and they can be used most successfully to complement modern interiors. The polyanthus are visually heavy enough here, but cowslips are too delicate.

Left: This handmade pot with its 'Celtic' pattern is an excellent choice for dried flowers. However, flower and design are both wrong here — the dried molucella is not only off-balance but too long for the vase.

TEXTURE AND CONTRAST

In flower arranging texture is as important as contrast. It is so easy to get carried away by including so many different textures in a design that in the end it lacks contrast.

In order to get the very best out of your materials, it is important to be aware not only of the individual character of flowers and foliage – their size, shape and colour values – but of their surface textures. Compare for instance, the texture of a rose with a carnation, a gazania with a chrysanthemum, or the shiny leaves of ivy with the dull fronds of grass. This will enable you to contrast rough with smooth, shiny with matt, plain with patterned and so on, to give a finer, more subtle dimension to your designs. It is worth looking out for this type of material and experimenting by contrasting texture with small and large, pointed with blunt or broad with narrow, to give an endless variety to all of your many designs.

Even within one flower there is variation in texture. The anemone-centred spray chrysanthemum, far right, has a knobby centre surrounded by a frill of smooth satiny petals. Like many other flowers, the passion flower, also, has its own built-in texture and contrast. The smooth outer circle of petals with a very fine fringed inner ring in purple, contrasts sharply with the cream.

The sameness of just carnations arranged in a round container as an all-round design (*top*) is spiced with gypsophila (*below*) — to give a softer, fuller effect with pleasing textural contrasts.

An interesting study in colour, line and texture (*right*). Notice how the rough weave of the container has been included in the design, and its low horizontal form balanced against the verticals and curves of the flowers.

All white flowers (*above*), each one different in texture size and shape, can become a challenging exercise. Two or three variations may give just the right balance to a design especially if it is complemented with suitable foliage. The permutations seem almost endless.

It is not easy to find a suitable container for these beautiful smooth anthurium flowers (*left*). Brass echoes the texture and shape and is visually heavy enough to underline the design.

WORLDWIDE INFLUENCES

Because communication is easy and people travel more, the interaction of one country on another in the field of flower arranging and also in professional flower design has never been more lively

Obviously, climate affects the availability of material for flower arranging. However, flowers can now be produced in quantity in controlled conditions and shipped world-wide, reaching the public in little more than 48 hours after they have been harvested. There is a vast choice of size, shape and colour; proteas and strelitzias, from Southern Africa, orchids from Australia and Singapore, carnations from the USA and South America, as well as huge quantities of fabric flowers and foliage from Hong Kong and Taiwan. These are only a few varieties that are now within every flower arranger's reach.

Records indicate that flowers and herbs have been cultivated in different countries throughout history not so much for decoration but for their medicinal properties. Thus gardens attached to religious institutions have always been efficiently cultivated, the herbs used as curatives while the vegetables fed the faithful.

The ancient Egyptians, Greeks, and Romans held flowers in high regard and many, such as the peony and lotus, were particularly significant.

But while interest in flower arranging in the West has really only accelerated since the Second World War, it is centuries old in Japan. The earliest known school of design was founded in a Kyoto temple by a Buddhist priest. The *Ikenobo* school has since flourished through 48 direct-line generations and today still specializes in the classic style of *Shoka* – a more modern interpretation of the old *Rikka*. The other two main schools of design in Japan were founded more recently. The *Ottara* school was founded in the nineteenth century and specializes in the *Moribana* style of design which is made in a shallow dish and the *Nagiere* style, which is made in an upright container. The *Sogetsu* school, the youngest of the three, emphasizes the beauty of colour while encouraging the unusual handling of materials. There are now more than 5,000 schools of design in Japan and teachers (flora ambassadors they could be called) have established branches in many other countries.

Returning to the West, there is little record of any design formula before 1940, when an American, J. Gregory-Conway, published his excellent book, *Flowers East-West*. This spells out design concepts which must surely have both enlightened and encouraged flower arrangers all over the world.

In Britain Violet Stevenson has written some very helpful books on flower arrangement in the early 1950s. Her awareness of the design potential of easy-to-grow garden flowers and wild material has, since then, influenced many professional and amateur designers.

Proteas (*left*) growing near Cape Town. These flowers will last for weeks if they are allowed to stand in water and can then be gradually dried, when they will retain their form but, unfortunately, lose some of their colour.
Above: A design from Korea, created for a grand environment. Interestingly, the material chosen — dahlias, astilbe and grasses — can also be found growing in the West.

A Japanese style arrangement (*above*) of three red carnations set vertically, one directly above the other. A few branches of berberis complete this strikingly simple design.

Strelitzias, named after King George III's Queen, are natives of South Africa. Here they are employed in a contemporary free-style arrangement of unusual colouring on a base of driftwood. Never crowd the long-lasting and very decorative strelitzia, and be sure they are really well conditioned.

The Japanese container, with its twisted cane handle, is a crucial part of the design (*above*). Soaked foam has been skewered with a wooden prong which rests across the mouth of the container and holds it in place.

DISPLAYING PLANTS

Arrangements are generally best when they are designed with a particular setting in mind.

If not, perfectly acceptable designs can be spoilt by their surroundings or backgrounds. However, this is not always obvious at the time. One way of dealing with this problem is to photograph the display, which will sometimes pinpoint any glaring errors of judgement.

The background colour is a common trap. Some colours will overpower the natural colours of the flower to a depressing degree while others will exaggerate them. Fabric textures will be emphasized and others not, particularly in a camera lens. But we are not speaking only of photographic effects because that is not usually the main purpose of a home arrangement. In any case, the eye does not

sometimes see things with as much clarity as the camera lens: the camera crystallizes the subject from one particular angle, whereas the beholder can move and adjust the subject to suit the eye.

It is advisable to experiment with both material and environment: that which is not pleasing in high summer may well be totally acceptable when the light value is low, or even in artificial light.

An example of parallel form design, suitable for a church or concert hall. Here, the flowers can be seen quite clearly but the shape of the arrangement is lost against the background. The green wall camouflages the foliage, and the broad yellow strip overpowers the parallel effect.

This beautiful arrangement provokes a question of balance and proportion. A tiny occasional table is hardly the correct base for such a large arrangement.

Geraniums can be wonderfully long-lasting flowers, but they will not survive for very long under a 100 watt reading lamp. Lighting can add drama and subtlety to designs, but see that the light source is well away from your flowers.

White and peach-coloured gladioli, carnations in a second shade of peach, yellow eremurus and blue delphiniums are the main ingredients of this very colourful display. It is a great temptation to put it on this wide window sill (*above*) with a beautiful view of the garden as backdrop. But it is a mistake — definition is entirely lost, and the sun shining through the glass will quickly burn the flowers.

It is not the line arrangement that is wrong (*left*), but the background. This warm orange would engulf almost any colour except white and certain complementary purples; and it is a particularly sad choice behind the peach colouring of the carnations and gladioli, which are drained of their subtlety.

The same arrangement placed against an attractive wallpaper (*above*), but the effect is one of contradiction. The wallpaper, in delicate coffee and cream tints, is fighting aggressively with the colourful floral design, and there are no winners.

Left: The plain background is a better choice, but almost every other feature of the positioning is wrong. Crammed between a lamp and a picture, on a narrow mantlepiece, the clear design appears confused and 'busy'; and when the lamp is on the flowers will be burned. A more pleasing setting would be a plain-coloured background with plenty of space around.

CHAPTER THREE

THE INFLUENCE OF COLOUR

To be able to maximize the quality of colour by understanding its tonal values, using them to achieve perspective, and therefore create a harmonious design, plays a crucial part in the success of any flower arrangement. However beautiful and brilliantly coloured your flowers might be, a discordant colour scheme can spoil the best arrangement. The complexities of local colour and their tonal values make fascinating study in themselves, and are even more rewarding when translated into flower arrangements. The following pages explain what tonal values are and how they work so that you are able to get the very best from your floral designs.

PRINCIPLES OF
COLOUR SELECTION

It is said that if you want to create a positive impression on your business associates, then have a red wall in your office. It is maintained that this colour will act as a backup to the executive aura. In addition to having a specific total value, each colour is said to have a connotation related to human reaction. Thus red is positive and signifies power. Blue is the most introvert colour and implies faith and sometimes meekness, even timidity. Orange is supposed to suggest pride in the nicest sense of the word, while violet denotes gentleness and piety. Green indicates sympathy and compassion, while white is the very essence of light and signifies purity.

The first step is to clarify the primary colours: they are red, yellow and blue. All other colours are made from these in varying degrees of intensity. The primaries can be mixed to produce secondary colours, for example, blue and red make violet, yellow and blue make green, while yellow mixed with red produces orange. You may wonder what this has to do with flower arranging since we cannot stir a yellow daffodil and a scarlet tulip together in a bowl and produce an orange lily. In flower arrangement it is a question of understanding the values of each colour we use in order to produce the effect we want. For example, a vase with seven scarlet tulips and three pale blue irises would not be at all impressive or interesting, as red is an extrovert dominant colour while blue is receding and gentle. In short, the irises would be totally swamped by the red flowers.

Undoubtedly, colour has a definite effect on our senses, so it is worth remembering that bright, striking effects can be made by using warm colours, such as red, orange and warm yellows (these are the advancing colours), while more soothing and delicate designs can be made by using cooler blue-pinks, mauves, blue and purple (these are the receding colours). Grey foliage can also be used in cooler arrangements.

An arrangement with varying levels of one colour, such as pale pink through to red, is described as being monochromatic. This category of colour harmony is usually very restful on the eye.

To choose any three neighbouring colours on the colour wheel, for example, from pink through red to mauve, will give you a harmonic colour scheme. In terms of flowers, this type of colour scheme is very pleasing indeed.

For a more striking effect, experi-

Lilac, liatris and berberis in a half-glazed Chinese ginger jar. Notice how the receding colour of the berberis emphasizes the flowers in this radiating design.

ment with complementary colour schemes. These are the colours that are directly opposite each other on the colour wheel, such as violet and yellow, blue and orange or green and scarlet. Do not necessarily choose the basic hue, but try to use

Too much of one type of material can be overwhelming. A vertical arrangement consisting of two varieties of lemon and yellow spray chrysanthemums needs another texture and colour to spice it up.

A 'cottage' arrangement (*above*) in a small mass-produced pottery pedestal. Red anemones, a little mauve honesty and a few brown spidery chrysanthemums are lifted from being too sombre by adding just a few bright yellow spray chrysanthemums.

Left: A contrast of texture is needed in this arrangement of spidery chrysanthemums, which looks slightly ragged and 'thin', without style or substance.

Colour Wheel

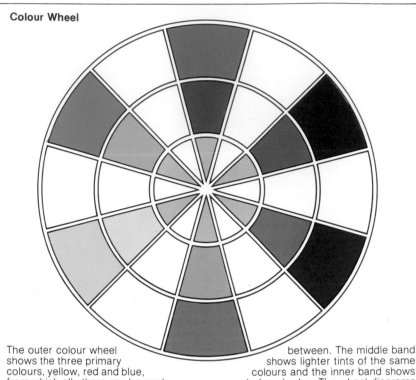

The outer colour wheel shows the three primary colours, yellow, red and blue, from which all others can be made, with secondary colours (pure hues) in between. The middle band shows lighter tints of the same colours and the inner band shows darker shades. The wheel diagrams below illustrate four basic colour schemes.

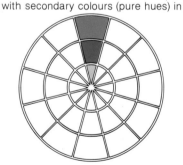

Monochromatic Shades and tints of any one single colour.

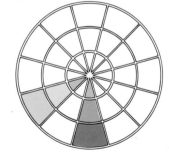

Harmonic Groups of any three or four colours lying next to each other.

Complementary Colours which lie opposite each other.

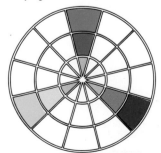

Triadic Any three colours lying at equidistant intervals.

tints and tones of each one. If you use them in well-balanced proportions you will produce very agreeable results.

One point to bear in mind with regard to colour in relation to living flowers is that their colours do change slightly every day. As the flower dehydrates, so the colour drains from it. Some flowers fade more noticeably than others, but in spite of their transient nature, we can enjoy them for as long as they have colour.

Lighting is very important in flower arranging – the colours of both flowers and foliage will look quite different if the arrangement is placed in a dark corner or on a window sill, or if it is seen under different types of electric light. Blue and mauve for instance, lose the crisp, clear colour that natural light gives them and become a rather dull grey under electric light. Fluorescent lighting, on the other hand, will enhance blue though it will make red appear a muddy brown. Tungsten lighting is appropriate for red, orange and yellow.

Daylight and electric light cast different shadows, so if you want your flowers to look their best under electric light, arrange them at a time when your choice of electric light is turned on.

The correct colour, form and texture will also give shape to a design. Colour perspective is built up by graduating and complementing the tonal value of each local colour. Light colours will stand out and become the focal point in your arrangement if you place material of a deeper tonal value behind them. Similarly you can use local colour that has lighter tones to soften and enhance colours that have darker tones.

The subtle use of local colour to create perspective in flower arranging is closely allied to techniques used by artists to give perspective to their paintings. Indeed, the artists of seventeenth- and eighteenth-century Dutch and Flemish flower paintings were instrumental in showing flower arrangers how emphasis and depth could be achieved in this way.

Here sharp colour contrasts emphasize the tonal value and details of the carnation.

Contrast between black and white is strong and makes the white flower stand out.

Similar tones of flower and background colours emphasize the yellow in the petals.

This green has a lighter tonal value than the second and creates a nearer image.

Here, the darker tone of green creates depth and the flower also recedes.

Green appears to emphasize the colour and contours of the carnation.

Detail and contrast are reduced because the tonal values are too similar.

The blue background recedes from the vibrant red carnation.

The yellow and red are both advancing colours with similar tonal values.

HARMONIZING
COLOURS

In flower arranging, harmony is almost as complex as it is in music. And 'that which forms a consistent or agreeable whole' must be our objective. We must not only use flowers and foliage that are in harmony from the point of view of colour, form and texture, but also in respect of the character of the material. Yes, flowers do have character: compare an arum lily with a violet; a daffodil with a rose.

The material must also harmonize with its container and its surroundings. For instance, a severe-line arrangement based in a wonderful silver dish intended as decoration for a brick fireplace in a sixteenth-century country cottage would not be in keeping with the background. A more simple style of design arranged in a copper or basketware container would be more in harmony with these rustic surroundings.

But always remember that in flower arranging, as in music, enjoyment of the end-product is the main aim, so do not be worried if your concept of harmony does not agree with other people's.

Magenta spray carnations (*above*) are an agreeable choice for the dull red of this rough-finish brick container, while sprays of honeysuckle blend the two colours together.

A charming old-world jug with a bouquet of anemones on the front (*below*) is the obvious container for these long-stemmed anemones. It is quite a luxury to find these flowers with such long stems, so the design was contrived to use as much of the stem and its natural curve as possible. These are arranged in a block of foam, which fits neatly into the neck of the jug.

This tall container (*above*) makes a lovely base for deep blue/mauve irises, pale mauve honesty flowers and pinky mauve freesias. The straight stems of the irises are set in symmetrically, while the honesty sprays provide a softer outline in contrast.

Left: Cerise spray chrysanthemums, pale pink spray carnations and alstroemeria almost exactly echo the colours of this old-fashioned water jug. The flowers are set in asymmetrical style, with a bold main line following the lip of the jug to the right.

CONTRASTING
ARRANGEMENTS

The term contrast, in the art of flower arranging, refers not only to colour, but also to form, texture and the individual character of the material. This means that you could have a design in monochromatic colours combined with contrasting shapes and texture.

Obviously, contrast also refers to colour and how drab life would be without it. But never confuse contrast with discord of any kind. Two synonyms of this word are strife and harsh, neither of which has any place in the flower arranger's dictionary.

In fact, contrast presents a challenge: it is relatively quick and easy to make a small design with one kind of flower in one colour. But as soon as you begin to add other subjects, then you need to evaluate how much, where and, indeed, if. Decisions have to be made all along the line, entirely on your own for, as with colour, no two people will agree one hundred per cent on any given balance of contrast.

An arrangement of antirrhinums in two colours (*right*). Alone, the yellow or pink would be bland, but the longer yellow stems, spiced with a smaller quantity of pink flowers on shorter stems create an agreeable contrast of colour. Rust coloured chrysanthemums complete the design.

Opposite: The vertical design of arum lilies (*left*) is a little unimaginative in this whitemilk glass container, and the texture of the flowers is very similar to the finish of the vase. *Centre*: Add five stems of column stock and a contrast in colour, form and texture is immediately introduced. This may prove too strong a contrast for some tastes, so several heads of lilac are added at the heart of the arrangement, providing a third variation in colour value and texture. *Right*: Close-up of lily and column stock. *Below:* A basket full of contrasts — wild flowers, florsts' flowers and garden flowers. And if the chrysanthemum is regarded as a winter flower, the arrangement is also a contrast of seasons, spanning spring, early summer and winter.

GROUPING
COLOURS

Any material that has been grouped together becomes more significant than if it were scattered.

One of the main points in grouping colours is to know where to place certain colours to give the best effect in both the design and its location. Lighter colours can be used as highlights or focal interest,

while darker colours can be used to give depth, or to accentuate lighter colours. Most colours are usually more lively if they are not grouped too evenly throughout an arrangement. Think of the design as if you were painting it. 'Paint in' one group of material at a time, leaving one or two stems for the finishing touches.

This tall, circular black container (*below*) is a lovely base for the multi-coloured arrangement of liatris, yellow iris, red anemones and yellow broom (cytisus). Notice how the colours of the larger central flowers are echoed around the edges with lighter-weight blooms.

Grouping your colours. Here the main lines or purple are set in position (*above*). They form two distinct groups which are linked together with a single bloom.

The addition of broom and iris echoes and expands the lines of liatris. The iris — a particularly lovely variety called Angel's Wings — is lemon with white tipped petals, which is less emphatic than plain yellow.

Parallel form (*below*). In this type of grouping the aim is to imitate nature by arranging the material such as it grows. Thus, the taller flowers remain on long stems, while shorter ones are placed exactly as they grow, giving an interesting balance of scale and proportion. The base is usually — as here — a shallow dish-like container, which is packed with foam and topped with fresh moss.

An all-yellow design is given a strong focal point by inserting a few stems of magenta stock into the centre (*above*).

MONOCHROMATIC
COLOURS

Mono means one, thus a monochromatic arrangement is a design of one colour only. First decide on the colour and then introduce all available tints and shades of the basic colour. Obviously, it is not possible to blend as an artist would mix paint on a palette, but flowers of the same hue and those which are lighter and darker than the chosen colour may be included.

They may be flowers of the same family, but they might also be varied, which would introduce a contrast in texture as well.

Monochromatic harmony is probably the most soothing of all colour

Purple liatris with paler coloured lilac are the main materials used in this monochromatic design. Liatris is used to establish the radiating lines, which are further emphasized by the rich deep purple tones of the foliage. The pale lilac on shorter stems is inserted at the base of the design.

combinations, for the eye and mind are not assailed by possibly conflicting tints. No two people see colour alike and what gives pleasure to one may not please another.

However, arrangements in monochromatic harmony – and here the word harmony is particularly appropriate – suggest peace and lack of conflict. Such arrangements are obviously very acceptable in hospitals or in any situation where a calm atmosphere should be preserved. The colour chosen should also be appropriate to the situation. For example, to take a bouquet of red carnations to someone who is ill in an attempt 'to cheer him up' will probably have the reverse effect, while deep pink or a soft clover colour might achieve success. Colour is a continually absorbing aspect of flower arranging and every combination presents both its problems and challenges.

Delphiniums are obvious flowers for monochromatic treatment as well as for perpendicular designs. They range from the palest blue to a really rich ultramarine, here underlined by the blue of the glass container. Foliage of contrasting shapes completes the arrangement.

FOLIAGE ARRANGEMENTS

Sometimes foliage is regarded as just a background material. It is, of course, indispensable both for masking the foam support and as a background for the flower arrangement. There are also several types of very distinctive foliage that can be designed without flowers, as mixed foliage arrangements in their own right. I remember a presentation given by an eminent Japanese designer living in Britain who used nothing but foliage in his designs, and yet none of the material was particularly rare. He created many delightful arrangements, some in the Japanese style and some in the Western style.

Foliage should, of course, be selected with as much care as flowers, keeping an eye on colour, shape and texture. There are leaves with a definite blue-grey tint, others with a yellow-cream bias, while some are grey or silver, to mention but a few. Most leaves condition well by being submerged for several hours in clear water. Examples that respond well to this technique are hosta, begonia rex and chlorophytum. Those leaves with a hairy or velvety texture should not be submerged, but should be stood in shallow water. Young leaves are quite charming, with their fresh green shapes, but unfortunately they do not last very long. Some, however, will enjoy being stood in a few inches of quite hot water, to which flower food has been added.

The enormous variety of flowers and foliage that blooms throughout the year, gives ample choice for planning a simple or elaborate arrangement, and for buying flowers to suit your budget.

A contrast in colour and shape, with the graceful feathery grevillea at the centre of this arrangement. A lovely dark red is introduced by the zebrina to the left, which makes an interesting contrast with the yellow/green variegation of peperomia on the right.

The material (*above*) chosen for a green arrangement is not strictly foliage alone since the seed heads of some bluebells have been included to vary texture.

Using these simple materials this arrangement (*right*) has been designed for all-round effect, with grasses forming a central line.

The delicately shaded green and cream vase with its slender neck is an obvious choice for a green arrangement. The bell-like flowers of the tolmica make an interesting contrast with the deep red fingers of the hellebore leaves and the feathery, downward-curving hedge parsley.

Further contrast has been added at the centre of the design on the left with the addition of hellebore flowers and the still-green flowers of the *Viburnum opulus* or snowball tree.

A third alternative. The hellebore flowers and *Viburnum opulus* have gone, and the deep red of the hellebore foliage is given prominence once more. Below, new contrast is provided with the introduction of four types of variegated leaf.

CHAPTER FOUR

USEFUL FLOWERS AND FOLIAGE FOR ARRANGING

One of the greatest joys of flower arranging is working
with the rich panoply of flowers, foliage and shrubs that each
season brings. Spring is heralded by colourful stretches of
woodland bluebells and a 'host of golden daffodils'.
Red poppies, cornflowers and the classic red rose are the
hallmarks of summer; autumn is announced by fiery coloured
foliage, feathery pampas grass and colourful cotoneaster, while
Michaelmas daisies, bright red holly berries and poinsettias
begin the season of winter.
This chapter explains fully how and when to cut flowers,
how to display them to their best advantage, and, most
important of all, how to make them last so that your
arrangements can be enjoyed to the full.

SPRING
FLOWERS

Spring flowers offer the flower arranger a fantastic range of materials, including colour, form and size – a complete palette from which to choose, mix, match and harmonize.

In the Northern Hemisphere, the daffodil is the true spring flower and, even though it can often be bought in flower shops well before Christmas, it is still thought of as the signal that winter is almost past. It is also one of the earliest-known flowers. Gerard, the herbalist writes in his first *Herball* of 1599, that Theocritus speaks of a 'nymphs idyll', describing maidens gathering sweetly-scented wild daffodils and hyacinths (presumably the early bluebell).

Daffodils are probably one of the most popular of flowers, for they are produced commercially in huge quantities out of their natural season, which means that, in cool climates, they can be enjoyed from early December through to March. For many years now daffodils have been sold in fairly tight bud as it was found that the flowers suffered less damage if they were harvested and packed at what is called the 'gooseneck' stage. That is, when the flower has turned downwards ready to show colour. To cut them before this stage would be too early and the flowers would not develop to their true size and beauty. Tulips, irises and freesias are also commercially packed in bud, as are many hybrid lilies such as the lovely orange Enchantment, clear yellow Destiny or Connecticut King, and the beautiful white variety called Juliana. They obviously travel better in bud and will open gradually to give a succession of flowers all on one stem.

If spring flowers are bought fresh from the florist, their conditioning is very simple. As a general rule, all bulb-grown flowers should be stood in only a small amount of water, about 3-4in (8-10 cm), to which flower food has been added. It is not always essential to cut the stems of daffodils, tulips or freesias, as they drink easily, and cutting the stem-end would cause the flower to open more readily.

Anemones, also, prefer a shallow amount of water. Most lilies usually have rather woody stems and these should be cut with a sharp knife before being conditioned in shallow flower-food solution. It is advisable to leave your spring flowers for an hour or so in as cool and dark a place as possible so that the stems can take up plenty of water. This will reward you with healthy-looking blooms and several days' longer vase life.

Tulips like to curve towards the light and frequently this adds movement and interest to a design. But if you want your tulips to stand upright, you may have to insert wires into their stems, taking care not to puncture them. Insert the wire upwards until you feel it come into contact with the seedbox inside the tulip. The flower should then remain nice and stiff. Polyanthus, like daffodils and tulips, look their best when arranged comparatively informally. Unlike most other flowers, they seem to prefer to be packed tightly into the vase. This does not sound like flower arranging at all, but usually when they are used singly, they hang their heads no matter how well they have been conditioned. Garden-grown lilies-of-the-valley are very similar in this respect, preferring to be 'arranged' in a close-packed, handmade bouquet and set into a narrow vase, rather than each stem being put in separately. All flowers enjoy an overhead spray with clear water after being arranged.

Try, whenever possible to use each flower's natural foliage for arranging. Tulips have plenty of leaves, as do irises and violets. Polyanthus leaves will droop unless they have been submerged in water for at least an hour, but after a good 'drowning' they will last just as long as the flowers.

The many beautiful spring-flowering garden shrubs are excellent for large arrangements. Sprays of bright yellow forsythia, delicate prunus, very early-flowering winter jasmine and 'fingers' of witch-hazel on bare branches will all mix happily, either with bulb-grown flowers or by themselves.

Tolmiea

Gerbera

Alyssum

Lily

Nettle (yellow archangel)

Carnation

Lily

Lilac

Iris

An arrangement in yellow and white: daffodils, narcissus and nettles in a crystal goblet bring all the freshness of spring into the living room.

Anemone

Hellebore

Broom

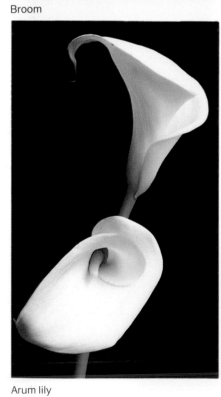

Daffodil

Arum lily

Liatris

Lily-of-the-valley

Japonica (Japanese quince)

Cowslip

Ixia

Anthurium

Freesia

SUMMER
FLOWERS

Summer brings an abundance of flowers in many varieties of size, shape and colour. Even if you do not have a garden, you can still plant flowers in window boxes, planters, and hanging baskets. As long as the plants have light, regular watering and feeding, they will reward you with as many blooms as they would in the garden.

It is a joy to be able to pick flowers from the garden, cutting them precisely when you want them and standing them in water before arranging them.

If there is a quantity of one sort, you can make a one-type flower arrangement with emphasis on line and shape. And if there are still too many, then they can be dried gradually for the winter months. If there are many different types of flowers all blooming at once you can mix them together, making sure that the smaller flowers are not overpowered by the larger varieties.

Before cutting the flowers, do remember to have a container with about 5in (13cm of water and flower food ready to put them in. In this way your flowers will last as long as possible. Summer storms can spoil lovely blooms, so sometimes it is better to bring them indoors rather than leave them to be beaten down by wind and rain.

Sedum

Philadelphus

Geranium

Delphinium

Antirrhinum

Molucella

Antirrhinum

Larkspur

Sunflower

Potato flower

A basket is an appropriate container for a mixture of summer flowers and foliage: different colours and textures, shapes and sizes, will all blend happily together. Be sure to condition all the material well. Poppies, for instance, will survive only a day or two, but are lovely while they last. Immediately after cutting, stand them in about 2in (5cm) of almost boiling water and leave them until the water cools. Then add them to the arrangement.

Summer flowers in a basket(*above*). A plastic saucer is attached to the basket with Oasis-fix and a fairly large piece of foam is impaled in an Oasis-prong in the saucer. Foliage is used to mask the foam.

Molucella is used to describe the maximum height and width of the design, while flower stems echo the main lines (*above*).

Grouped flowers balance the foliage and one huge garden rose is set towards the middle of the design (*above*).

Right: The finished arrangement. Strong touches of colour have been added to the main vertical and horizontal lines. Normally, no material should be placed higher than the handle, but the rule is broken here to suit the overall effect of a colourful summer garden.

Rose

Allium

Alchemilla

Pansy

Geranium

Hypericum

Lupin

Strelitzia

Double poppy

Eremurus

Phlox

Foxglove

Rhododendron

Marigold

Clarkia

Clematis

Cymbidium

Candytuft

Geranium

Single poppy

Candytuft

Hydrangea

Sweet william

Sweet pea

Loosestrife

Chrysanthemum

Oriental poppy

Dianthus

Roses and their sweet-scented perfume epitomize summer. One of the happiest sensations for the keen gardener and flower arranger is picking the first bud of the season and watching it expand.

In his *Herball* of 1599, Gerard observes that although the rose is 'a shrub full of prickles', yet it should not be planted amongst other shrubs but given a place of honour amongst the 'most glorious flowers of the world'.

A magnificent silver wedding gift (*above*). White roses in this elegant silver container make a most impressive design. Arranged in an almost free-style open fan shape with their own foliage, the flowers are set into an inner container to protect the silver.

A colourful display of red, orange and yellow roses (*left*) with a light edging of pale green fern. Notice the contrasting curve of the container.

The rose is not only one of the most beautiful of shrubs, offering a great variety of shapes, colours and sizes, it is also extremely hardy. It will bloom in what seem quite inappropriate situations where lesser flowers might just die.

From the arranger's point of view, roses are particularly adaptable: they are ideal for gifts, bridal bouquets, table centrepieces – and one perfect bud on a gift-wrapped parcel makes it look twice as special. Roses are also suitable for funeral and sympathy tributes and for buttonholes; while for a dedicated flower arranger, the gift of a new variety for the garden makes a wonderful present, for it is hoped that no garden is so well stocked that there is no space for another variety of rose.

Roses also look good in almost any kind of container.

AUTUMN
FLOWERS

This is the season of mists and mellow fruitfulness, with string beans, blackberries and grapes – hanging thick and black patiently waiting to be made into wine; bright orange Chinese lanterns (physalis), multi-coloured statice and honesty 'moons', and the pinky-mauve fingers of autumn crocus (colchicum), which seem to shoot up when least expected. There are also Michaelmas daisies and dahlias. These are just some of the flowers that provide us with material for autumn arrangements.

The whole dahlia family offers a fantastic choice of colour, shape and size. It includes huge decorative blooms the size of a dinner plate, the medium-sized pom-pom variety, the spiky cactus type and the really tiny button dahlias which, incidentally, make perfect buttonholes, while the creamy white variety make ideal yet simple bridal bouquets. Even though dahlias, and many other flowers, are circular, a line effect can be achieved by carefully grading the colour and size. Try to use each flower the way it faces naturally and profit by any curving stem that will emphasize your line. Remove most of the foliage, for however much one enjoys leaves, dahlia foliage is not always very decorative and it does need a lot of water. Side buds should be cut off and inserted on their own stems. If left on the main stem, they will quickly droop.

Sedum

Erigeron

Statice

Gladiolus

Below: The warm golden colours of autumn are reflected in this asymmetrical arrangement of yellow cactus and orange and red pompom dahlias. The container, an unusual pottery jug, forms a perfect contrast to the rather busy texture of the flowers. The stems are set in soaked foam and the whole arrangement can be gently lifted out in order to add more water. This should be done frequently since dahlias are greedy drinkers.

Physalis

Cactus and pompom dahlias

WILD
FLOWERS

Many wild flowers although generally more delicate than garden varieties are undoubtedly worth picking and arranging. They will need careful conditioning, but before that they should be protected from the sun and wind as soon as they are collected. It is the sun and wind that absorb moisture from around the flowers.

So often one sees wild flowers and by the time they can be conditioned they are almost past redemption. It is a good idea to take with you a small knife and several plastic bags, even a jar or two with a little water, whenever possible. A large spray will also help to keep the flowers reasonably fresh until they can have a proper drink. Many wild flowers will respond well to being stood in quite hot water, while foliage and large stems should be submerged for up to 12 hours, after which time they will be quite strong and ready to be arranged.

Plan your wild flower designs in the same way as other garden flowers – picking only those you require. Do not over-pick and remember it is illegal to collect protected species.

A free arrangement of wood-sorrel, speedwells and buttercups in a clear glass jar (*above*). No need for foam here — the flowers are simply grouped and set in the jar to be held in place by its slender neck.

Bluebells (*left*), the delicate spring flowers of the woodlands, can bring a reminder of the countryside into your home.

Vinca major and stitchwort in a handmade pottery vase (*above*). Even when rushed into water as soon as it is cut, vinca will not last more than two days, but is is a lovely colour and looks very appealing in free arrangements of this kind.

Left: A free-style arrangement of wild parsley and a little pale mauve honesty in a basketware base decorated with a piece of contorted willow. A plastic container, prepared with a prong and a piece of soaked foam, is attached to the basketware base with Oasis-fix. The willow branch is attached to the foam by two wire 'legs'. The design is built up using the same technique as for more formal material, establishing one line at a time with a single type of flower.

The soft yellow heads of cowslips (*right*) will add a bright touch to wild flower arrangements in early summer. These flowers are rare in some areas and should not be picked.

The jam jar technique (*above*), and a more carefully considered grouping in a glass ginger jar (*right*). The latter, still fresh and informal, takes very little more time. No foam is required as the neck of the ginger jar is sufficiently slim to hold the material in place.

A white variety of the bluebell (*right*) can sometimes be found growing in the wild. Occasionally, too, it can be bought at florists.

The flowers shown opposite now arranged in a basket (*above*). They have been conditioned in a flower food solution, which should be used for all material including wild flowers, making them tolerant of insertion in soaked foam. The foam is attached to prongs in a plastic container, which is secured to the basket base by Oasis-fix. There is no space for water in a shallow container such as this, but if the foam is soaked thoroughly and the block is sprayed daily, the flowers will last well.

INDOOR PLANT ARRANGEMENTS

Even if you have no garden, you can create several indoor gardens in miniature, designing each one as a cameo. Plants that might never tolerate varying weather conditions will burgeon and flower, even out of season, in homes, offices and shops.

However, plants in general do require light above all else. It is rather tempting to put flowers and plants in places where they will 'add a touch of colour', perhaps in a hallway or in a room well away from the window. They will tolerate such conditions for a short time, but eventually they will become straggly in their vain attempts to get more light, or they may just collapse and die. When in doubt, do enquire at your local garden centre or nursery, or consult one of the many plant books now available.

Plants on their roots arranged in a suitable container are known as 'planted bowls'. The bowl should be large enough for the roots, with a little extra space for them to grow. Strictly speaking, the base at least ought to be non-glazed. If your container is totally glazed, then put more 'crocks' or tiles at the base and water a little less. Try to extract the plant from its original pot neatly, keeping the root system intact. If you have to work indoors, remember to spread some plastic or sheets of newspaper, not only to protect the surroundings, but also to gather up any excess potting compost that can be used on another occasion.

Before you begin, place the plants in the bowl to decide how you want them to look, the tallest plant in the centre or to one side. If there is a trailing plant, this will probably be set towards the edge. Putting a bowl together for visual appeal is not very different from planning a flower arrangement: you have size, shape and form of material, and colour. Consider whether it is going to be a seasonal planting or a longer term design. For example, a bowl of hyacinths or crocuses will obviously last only while the flowers bloom, but one planted with green plants may last for some years.

Create a dish garden with plants –

An indoor garden in a pottery dish (*top*) with pelargonium, purple streptocarpus, shiny-leaved iresine and ivy foliage. The earth is topped with moss. This is a charming study of complementary reds and greens, excellent contrasting contours and variegated leaves.

1 To make an indoor garden, first lay broken crocks in the base of a container, and add soil and some water. Then begin to build up your design.

2 To add flowers, fix wire or a fine cane to the base of some florist's tubes with adhesive tape, add water and push the tubes into the soil.

3 Give the finished design a final watering. The character of the design can be changed from time to time, and the three stems of antirrhinum, which give extra height in this arrangement, can be replaced by other flowers in season.

usually fairly short-term ones – set in a shallow container. A miniature rock-garden, for example, could be created in this way. So, for comparatively little time and money, anyone can have a colourful indoor garden. A word of warning: it is fine to put your flowering dish garden or planted bowl on the window sill during the winter so that it gets maximum light, but unless you have double glazing, do not leave it there during the night. The cold air will stream down the glass and may have the same effect as a frost.

PLANT SUGGESTIONS

Here are a few suggestions for indoor plants whose foliage will add character to your arrangements. One or two leaves taken carefully from a plant will not materially alter its decorative value, but it is wise to cut carefully, particularly during the winter. Foliage cuts like this will also need good conditioning before being used and most varieties will enjoy being immersed in water for at least four hours.

Asparagus fern Several varieties are both easy to grow and decorative. *Var. sprengeri* throws beautiful long tails.

Chlorophytum The spider plant; not only are the leaves very decorative but the little 'spiders' can be set into the heart of an arrangement to great effect.

Codiaeum or Croton Very colourful and quite strong.

Dieffenbachia picta Known as dumbcane. Be careful not to get the sap near your eyes.

Maranta tricolor The prayer plant.

Begonia rex Extremely decorative and strong; there are several significant varieties.

Euonymus japonicus Will tolerate being planted outside in the south and west of Britain to grow larger and give you more colourful branches.

Ficus radicans Trailing fig; does not bear fruit.

Hedera There are many attractive varieties as well as the dark green hedge ivy that gives you long trails for large designs almost any time of the year.

Hypocyrta glabra The clog plant.

Nephrolepis The Boston fern. A special variety called 'Fluffy ruffles' is really lovely and full of character.

Pellea rotundifolia The button fern.

Peperomia magnoliaefolia Desert privet; leaves are very long lasting.

Phyllitis Hart's tongue fern, fine for emphasis.

Plectranthus Swedish ivy with interesting trails.

Scindapsus aureus You can 'steal' several leaves from a mature plant, which may make all the difference to your arrangement. The leaves have fairly long stems which is another plus.

Synhonium Sometimes known as Nephthytis or the arrowhead plant, its leaves are large and very decorative.

CHAPTER FIVE

SPECIAL
OCCASIONS

Half the fun of arranging flowers is to make a design
to celebrate a special occasion, and this is when the flower
arranger's creativity is put to the real test and when it will
be most admired.
The information given on the following pages explains
how to make wedding bouquets, head-dresses and posies,
and how to wrap a gift bouquet. Also included are ideas
for table decorations, hints on how to decorate a prayer book,
flower designs most appropriate for weddings and christenings
and for church decoration.

TABLE
DECORATIONS

Table decorations can range from really simple styles, with just a few flowers picked from the garden and put in water, to full-coloured, elaborately shaped confections.

The Victorians greatly favoured the epergne. These branched edifices, often made from silver and crystal, were used to grace their dinner tables. They were lavishly decorated with fruit and flowers, usually from the family's hothouses. Very large tables would have several of these confections, and since the material was not concentrated in one place, it would not inhibit lively, across-the-table conversation. This is one of the main points to bear in mind when making your table decoration. It should not be so big as to block the view nor should it be out of scale with the setting.

1 To make a table centrepiece, mark five lateral points with lily-of-the-valley foliage and mask the foam with molucella and hellebore leaves.

2 Having marked the tallest point with one stem of spray chrysanthemums, cut 5 stems of the same type of chrysanthemum to one length and 15 of the spidery variety.

3 Form the outer edge of the design with 5 of the spidery blooms and place the rest towards the centre to take colour and texture inwards.

4 The finished design (*right*) with single chrysanthemums added between the spidery blooms at the centre, to give a contrast both in tone and texture while using the same type of flower in the same colour.

An unusual centrepiece of fruit and flowers (*right*). At the centre of each layer is a piece of soaked foam on prongs, into which laurel leaves have been inserted with a sharp knife. Before insertion, the leaves, cut with as much stem as possible, were first cleaned with damp absorbent paper, sprayed to give them a sheen and left to dry for a few moments. The flowers for the top of the design were well-conditioned, their stems cut to a sharp angle and the middle ones left on slightly longer stems than the surrounding ones to create the neatly tapered outline.

This charming design in pink and white (*left*) uses carnations and lilies with an edging of gypsophila arranged in an elegant green glass vase.

WEDDING BOUQUETS
AND POSIES

All brides deserve lovely flowers for their special day. But never be confused by the vast choice of style and colour, for, while the materials will vary considerably from season to season, the basic shapes remain constant. First of all, decide what type of bouquet you would like, and, if possible, plan the colour and shape of the bridesmaids' flowers and any table decorations at the same time. In this way, all the wedding floral decorations will harmonize. Originally, all bouquets were loose natural bunches or tightly-packed nosegays simply tied and held in the hand. In the late eighteenth and early nineteenth centuries they became very large and very heavy. Presumably this was in line with the upsurge of interest in horticulture at the time when many more foliages were available and some brides were almost submerged by cascades of ferns.

However, in the early 1950s, bouquets began to diminish in size and the technique of making them became far more precise and delicate. Many were miniature works of art. Professional designers were able to do this type of work because they had access to better materials – finer wires, different coloured binding tape and ribbons in a multitude of colours, widths and designs.

Even so, the basic form was much the same. That is, flowers on single stems or taped 'stems', built into a design that could comfortably be held in one hand.

A classic shower or waterfall shape is still very popular. It is adaptable to almost any type of flower, is easy to hold and looks elegant.

The semi-crescent design is an extremely graceful bouquet. It is just as effective with simple flowers on their natural stems as with 'special wedding' flowers which have to be wired into trails.

The full-crescent is another popular variation, particularly suitable to accompany brides with long, full-skirted gowns.

Whether the bouquet has ribbon trails or not, it should always be neatly finished at the back with a small bow and a comfortable ribbon handle.

The classic style, unashamedly expensive when made up in lily-of-the-valley, stephanotis and white roses. These are all traditional bridal flowers, but there is no reason why the same shape should not be copied in many other flowers.

1 To wire and tape a hollow-stemmed flower, first cut your stem to the required length and then carefully insert a piece of wire through the stem and centre of the flower.

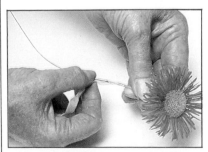

2 Using florist's tape and starting about ½ in (15mm) up the stem, bind both the stem and wire together and continue binding until they are covered.

A tiny baskette or bascade (*top right*) which is, in effect, two large corsages with very long handles which are covered with ribbon and joined firmly together at the centre.

Top left: A classic style bouquet composed of seven orange gerbera, each of them supported by an internal wire. Five bergenia leaves underline the central point, and three gerbera 'stems' have been added to create an impression of a semi-natural group.

Above: A full-crescent bouquet of spray chrysanthemums, underlined with gold braid loops of varying sizes. The flowers have conveniently hollow stems so that a fine supporting wire can be inserted without damaging the flower.

Two semi-crescent bouquets. *Above*: An all foliage bouquet, which can be made at any season with any type of leaf that will tolerate being carefully wired and left out of water for several hours. A foliage bouquet can appear rather flat unless something with volume, such as the green flower head here, is included.

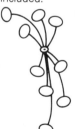

Right: Green cymbidium orchids and foliage. Each leaf is wired separately, taped and then built into trails.

All the flowers are on their natural stems in this hand posy so that it can be placed in water. To make the posy, take three strips of tulle, one shorter than the other two, and gather them on wire to form circles. Place a few flowers inside the smallest frill and pull the wire tight (though not so tight that the stems break). Then, randomly position flowers around it, gather the second frill around the bunch and pull the wire tight. Position the remaining flowers followed by the third frill. Pull this last wire tight and add ribbon trimming.

The bridal bouquet will, of course, be lovely: the bridesmaids and flower girls complete the wedding picture. Happily, there is a wide selection of flowers and designs for them to choose from.

Bascades resemble baskets of flowers (although they are actually designed like small bouquets with a ribboned handle), and they can be copied in any size to suit both child attendants and taller bridesmaids. A head-dress to match, in either real or fabric flowers, completes the effect.

Pomanders (floral balls) can also be

designed in several sizes. The ribbon handle is, of course, graded in length according to the height of the bridesmaid. Both these and the bascades are popular with the younger attendants as they can be swung around without damaging the flowers! Sometimes a wedding ceremony can prove a bit overwhelming for young bridesmaids.

For a country wedding, pomanders made with wild flowers such as marguerites (moon daisies) would look absolutely enchanting. Or maybe the bridesmaids would prefer to carry natural posies of mixed flowers. If the flowers seem limp after the wedding, immerse the bouquet completely in cold water overnight. They will, no doubt, revive and last for several more days.

Left: A sandalwood fan decorated with a small corsage of green Singapore orchids.
Above: A floral pomander made of tiny tulle bows decorated with a fresh flower spray.

Stitching and wiring ivy: Ivy is very long-lasting, so naturally it is quite popular for bridal designs. Every single leaf must be stitched with a fine silver wire and each 'stem' neatly bound with florist's tape. The tape is not only used for a neat finish, but to seal the base of the leaf or flower stem, thus keeping in any moisture and consequently helping material to last a little longer.

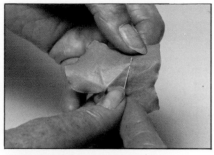

1 Select a sufficient number of clean, well-shaped leaves. Using a needle threaded with fine silver wire, make a small stitch at the centre back of an ivy leaf.

2 Carefully pull the wire thread through and, keeping the wire loop quite loose, lay one end down the side of the ivy stem and wind the other round both of them.

3 Next, starting at the base of the leaf, begin to bind the wire and ivy stem together with florist's tape.

4 Continue binding the wire 'stem' with florist's tape until your stem is the required length.

5 Several 'stems' of ivy can now be bound together and assembled into trails. These can be shaped to form part of your wedding bouquet.

WEDDING HEAD-DRESSES AND PRAYER BOOK

Instead of the traditional wedding bouquet, some brides prefer to carry a white bible or prayer book, with a small spray of flowers attached.

In effect, the spray follows the same kind of design as a bouquet and should be made in proportion to the size of the book. If it is too large, the whole effect is lost.

Ribbon markers are a matter for personal preference. One is usually passed through the page at the beginning of the Marriage Service and the other across the inside of the cover. These ribbons can look very attractive either left plain or decorated with tiny fresh flower heads.

For a summer country wedding, flower-decorated parasols would make charming accessories for the bridesmaids. They are quite lightweight to carry and can be closed for the ceremony. This should have no effect on the flower trimming providing it is done carefully. It is, of course, advisable to let your florist know that you would like the parasol to be used both open and closed and then the trimming can be arranged accordingly.

This classic head-dress (*right*) is attached to a small hair comb. You can secure it with silver wire or with clear adhesive.

Whenever possible match head-dresses with bouquets and posies. This is particularly effective with a period design as shown in the Victorian posy and head-dress (*left and right*). The bridesmaid's posy and circlet are made of fabric flowers. The circlet is secured to the hair with hair grips (bobby pins).

There is a fairly wide range of bridal parasols (*above*) to choose from, and trimmings can be simple or elaborate. White is ideal for a prayer book spray (*above right*) and different flowers make an interesting contrast. Anchor the spray firmly to the prayer book (*right*) so that it fits closely to the cover.

WEDDING CAKE DECORATION
AND CAR BOUQUET

If possible, the bridal cake top should match, or at least blend with, some of the flowers in the bridal bouquet. If the bouquet is made with large flowers, such as red roses, then obviously this is not feasible, but sometimes a flower can be diminished by using just a few petals and joining them in small trails as mini-flowers.

You could even place a favourite vase on top of the cake and create a design on natural stems if the flowers are suitable. The cake top design should be kept as delicate as possible and in proportion to the size and height of the cake.

Decorating the bridal car can also contribute to the festivity of the occasion. The Oasis company has produced a suction base called an auto-corso which can be arranged in exactly the same manner as a horizontal-style flower arrangement. There can be no damage to coachwork as the base is rubber. The decoration can be fixed either to one wing, or to the bonnet, attached to water-resistant ribbons stretched from either side of the windshield. Decidedly a fun addition to the bridal flowers.

Horizontal-style flower arrangement for the wedding car (*below*) built on an 'auto-corso' base.

The auto-corso has a suction base (*above*) on which soaked foam is secured (*left*).

The cake top (*above*) is designed to match the all-white classic bouquet on page 92. Built in accordance with the five-point motif, all the wire 'stems' are bound at one point and then bound together to form one stem that neatly fits into the silver vase.

A two-tier cake with a small top decoration in fabric freesias and tiny daffodils, further emphasized by trailing ribbons and bows held at the four corners of the base.
The detail of the decoration (*left*) shows ribbon bows with a single daffodil simply arranged at each corner.

FLOWERS
FOR CHRISTENINGS

A christening is yet another happy occasion made more festive with plenty of flowers. What better first gift could a child have than to be surrounded by loving family and flowers?

As well as a pedestal design – or several if the church is large enough – you could have ceremonial brass candle-stands which look lovely when specially dressed for the day.

Use long-lasting flowers, if possible, rather than delicate varieties, and make sure your foam is well soaked because sometimes it is not practical to fix a container to the stand. There is generally a small rim around the candle, presumably to catch the wax; but it is sometimes poss-

ible to fit pieces of floral foam to both sides of the candle. It is advisable to seek permission from whoever is in charge before doing this, however.

Nowadays christenings are conducted within the framework of a church service, not as isolated services. This means, of course, that not only the immediate family but everyone else can enjoy the extra special flower decorations.

Do try to check them a day or so afterwards; nothing looks worse than special arrangements that are fading. No doubt the pedestals and vase designs will last, but try to ensure that everything else is cleaned up and tidied away as soon as it is past its best.

1 To decorate a cradle (available from the florist in a choice of pink, blue or white), fix a flat disc of soaked floral foam to a prong set in the cradle. A second round of foam will be needed to achieve the right height, which should be impaled on the first one with fine cane.
2 Define the basic shape with white ixia and cream altroemeria. Insert the stems laterally.
3 Add five stems of freesia and a pink ribbon to finish.

Left: White longiflorum lilies, white spray single chrysanthemums and some shapely sprays of white broom dress the Christening candle. Add a white ribbon for this very special occasion.

A simple three-point design with long-stemmed, yellow and white lilies (*left*). Delicate, drooping yellow fronds fill the central area.
Above: For a more special and festive effect gypsophila may be added. This is the same arrangement with a lavish quantity added.

CHURCH DECORATION

It is quite a responsibility as well as a pleasure to arrange flowers for a particular church festival: Easter, Harvest Festival, Christmas or a wedding.

After the weeks of Lent with no flowers at all, the church can be decorated for Easter as lavishly as time, material and money will permit. Daffodils are usually in abundance together with the new foliage. Many couples who marry at Easter have an extra lovely setting for their wedding.

Lilies are the traditional Easter flower and some churches prefer arums. These certainly are beautiful but are not easy to arrange because of their broad stems. Fortunately, though, they are entirely tolerant of being arranged in foam, providing it is possible to add more water to the container every alternate day or so.

The longiflorum and regale varieties have thinner, more woody stems and are much easier to arrange. They last just as well and also tolerate being arranged in foam providing the water level can be checked from time to time. These lilies are usually transported when they are very young, before the flowers open, to prevent them from being damaged. So buy them at least by the beginning of Easter week so that they can develop and show some bloom (as opposed to green buds) by the time you want to arrange them.

3 Insert the main lines of this three-point design first, well back in the foam. The side view shows these first stems in place, leaving the centre of the foam clear.

The Paschal candle, decorated with beautiful arum lilies for Eastertide. Notice the candle gives height to this classic design.

1 To make a church decoration, choose a deep bowl and fill it with foam. The second part-block is attached with adhesive tape. Use pieces of stem to prevent tape from cutting into the foam.

2 For such a large design, add a third smaller block of foam to the base, again setting stems in position to protect the foam, and securing it firmly with tape.

4 Add more stems, still as far back in the block as possible. See that they do not 'march forward' as this picture indicates, since this will result in a stodgy-looking effect and may upset the balance as well.

5 The completed design of daisies, lilies and broom. A classic example of a well proportioned design of white with a softening of yellow.

MAKING
A GIFT BOUQUET

Bouquets wrapped in clear cellophane with bright, richly looped bows suggest glamour, success, honour and royal occasions. To add such a touch of glamour to a bouquet of flowers from your own garden or from the florist is not difficult and is worth the effort.

You will need cellophane paper, a generous length of water-resistant ribbon and a staple gun. If you can plan ahead, it is well worth having an idea of the colour combination you want in your bouquet before you choose the ribbon, and you can then either match one of your colours or perhaps pick a ribbon that makes a strong contrast. Follow the instructions (*right*) and you will be able to add a touch of luxury to a gift of flowers.

1

2

1 To wrap a gift bouquet, first make sure that all stems of both flowers and foliage are clean and free from thorns or odd leaves. Then arrange the flowers and foliage as attractively as possible, longer stems to the back, keeping the shorter ones to the front. Try not to cut stems any shorter than absolutely necessary.
2 Tie the bouquet together at a comfortable tying point with a multi-loop bow of water-resistant ribbon, which has been tied across the centre with a fairly long piece of the same ribbon. It is a good idea to prepare the ribbon at the start. The bouquet should then be laid on the cellophane leaving enough paper to wrap the stems at the bottom and to fold over the flower heads.

The diagram shows the bouquet tied with ribbon and lying on cellophane paper. The arrows indicate how the paper should be folded over the stems and flower heads and tucked underneath the bow. The curved black arrows show how the ties should first be crossed at the back before the final bow is made at the front.

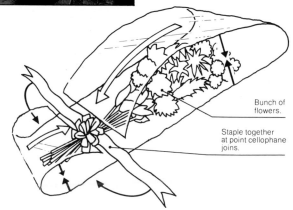

Bunch of flowers.

Staple together at point cellophane joins.

3 Arrange the cellophane over the flowers and stems so that the ends meet at the tying point. (About twice the length is enough.)
4 Then staple once each side at the tying point, keeping the cross ties outside the paper.
5 Cross the ties at the back and bring around to the front, finishing off with another bow across the centre of the first bow. Staple the edges at least twice, but to prevent the inside from steaming up, be careful not to overseal.

The finished gift bouquet of mixed garden flowers wrapped in cellophone paper and tied with a bright, contrasting bow.

WEDDING ANNIVERSARIES

Flowers make welcome gifts for wedding anniversaries, and it is worth taking trouble with decorative centrepieces for anniversary parties.

For this Golden Wedding arrangement, you will need to buy candles and several yards of net. Be generous with the net so that the pleating on each layer can be deep and the finished effect full. You will also need three circles of soaked foam of different sizes, and these should, if possible, be foam and polystyrene posy pads, which can be cut to the diameter you require. Gold spray will be needed to spray the candles, net and foam. The base is made from $\frac{1}{2}$in (15mm) thick wood or cardboard, covered with gold paper.

The all-round point method is used for inserting the flowers, with seven points for the first layer, five for the second and three for the top.

Fifth wedding anniversary gift (*above*). An outsize wooden spoon and fork decorated with a large spray of green Singapore orchids and hellebore seedheads, which are tied with nut-brown and pale brown ribbon.

1 If you cannot buy gold candles, any colour can be sprayed with gold paint. Remember to spray well away from the flowers.

2 The candles should be fitted with wire 'legs' and inserted in the top layer of foam. Pin a strip of gold paper or ribbon around the foam.

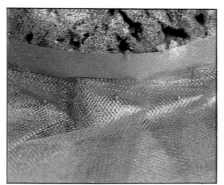

3 Pin pleated net to each layer of foam, attaching it to the covered base, and then spray with gold paint.

4 Insert mixed foliage and flowers in the first layer, using the all-round point method. Remember that all the material in the first stage is set in laterally.

5 Insert flowers and foliage into second layer, keeping the stems shorter to maintain the cone effect. Fix them firmly in place.

6 Do the same with the third layer, inserting the candles and finishing off the top with more flowers arranged to form the point of the cone.

ANNIVERSARIES

Most people will probably know that 25 years of marriage means a Silver Wedding anniversary, 40 years a Ruby celebration, and 50 years a Golden Wedding. All are milestones that should be marked with flowers and other appropriate gifts, and you may also wish to do the same for the ones in between.

1st: Paper	14th: Ivory
2nd: Cotton	15th: Crystal
3rd: Leather	20th: China
4th: Flowers	25th: Silver
5th: Wood	30th: Pearl
6th: Candy	35th: Coral
7th: Wool	40th: Ruby
8th: Pottery	45th: Sapphire
9th: Willow	50th: Gold
10th: Tin	55th: Emerald
11th: Steel	60th: Diamond
12th: Silk	70th: Platinum

7 Completed design for a Golden Wedding party.

BASKET ARRANGEMENTS

For many types of flowers, a basket would seem to be the natural container to choose. They are traditional containers, and have for centuries been used all over the world, for carrying such things as bricks, food, clothing, wood, indeed, all things domestic. Now they are designed specifically for flowers, and are available in a vast range of shapes and sizes from huge curved display baskets to shallow 'Nell Gwyn' shapes, all woven in beautiful natural colours. Wicker and cane can of course be spray-painted to match or complement the arranged flowers and the ribbon for the handle and bows.

They provide endless possibilities for decoration. The materials used to make baskets seem to look right almost anywhere as there is no really strong colour to conflict with existing interior decor. In addition to large arrangements for wedding parties, smaller arrangements can be carried by bridesmaids. They are also suitable for presentation to a visiting dignitary, for example, or for sending to a sick friend in hospital, where the flowers, if properly conditioned, will remain fresh for several days.

Perhaps a special gift might be included with the flowers such as fruit for someone in hospital, a few plants for a keen gardener, an Easter egg, or a bottle of perfume. Even if gift-wrapped separately, none of these would seem half so glamorous as when they are included in a basket of flowers.

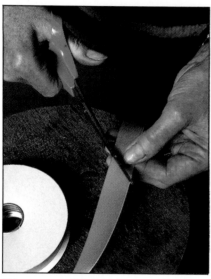

1 To prepare a basket, choose a ribbon that will harmonise with your proposed design and cut a generous length for binding the basket's handle (about 2-3 times the length will be sufficient).

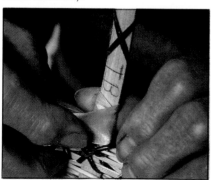

2 Attach the ribbon securely to the base of the handle with adhesive tape and begin binding.

3 To ensure that the binding does not slip after completion, keep the ribbon pulled taut as you wind. When the handle is covered, secure the end with adhesive tape.

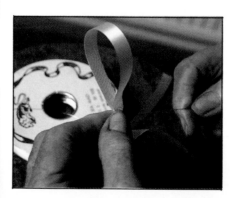

4 With a length of the same coloured ribbon, make a multi-looped bow, keeping the ends long for tying on to the basket.

5 Bind the ends of the ribbon round the centre of the bow and basket handle and tie firmly.

6 Now attach a prong to the inner plastic container with Oasis-fix and place two generous pieces of Oasis-fix on the base of the container.

A shallow basket filled with flowers of a variety of colours. The contrasting wicker handle is interesting enough without the addition of ribbon and would, in any case, prove difficult to bind neatly.

7 Attach the container to the basket. The whole base will be much firmer if you can now leave it to harden for at least a few hours before beginning your design.

9 Surround the base with a bed of moss, neatly masking the base sides.

11 Begin by inserting yellow tulips, which have been chosen as line flowers. Place tulip buds low down on the basket, placing the well-opened flowers in the middle of the arrangement.

8 Impale a soaked foam block on the prongs. this may be sufficient to hold your design, but if the flowers are heavy or the basket is to be transported, secure firmly with more layers of adhesive tape.

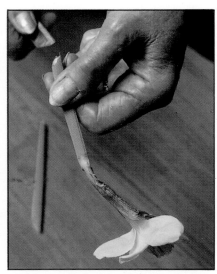

10 Next, take the flowers, remembering to cut the stems to a very sharp point so that they drive crisply into the foam.

12 The insertion of the tulips is now completed. Add some foliage, including both tulip and daffodil leaves, between the flowers as a background for the next selection of flowers. (*continued*)

13 Insert ten daffodils to echo the main lines and establish the height of the arrangement.

14 Position the daffodils so that the angle of each head forms a series of flowing lines around the basket edge.

15 Add small groups of gypsophila stems to fill the spaces between the flowers.

16 The completed basket (*right*) to which red alstroemeria has been added to give colour and character to the design.

CHRISTMAS DECORATIONS

Christmas celebrations as we know them today are based on nineteenth-century tradition. They are now so much a part of our life-style that it is difficult to realize that the tree with its trimmings and decorations, candles, cones and fruits, foliage, baubles and glitter, have been in fashion for a little over a hundred years.

The evergreen Christmas tree is the symbol of life and survival. It symbolises the changing of the seasons: its roots, flowers and fruit forming a continual life-cycle.

Candles are also symbolical of life, but in a less infinite way: that is, the lighted candle burns to its end in less than one day. Those countries that celebrate Christmas during the coldest and darkest time of year have good reason to enjoy the Christmas tradition, particularly since it is so near the shortest day which is another reason to enjoy preparing for the festivities: unfortunately, candles nowadays are substituted for winking electric lights, and the traditional fruits and nuts for glass baubles.

The door wreath is also a symbol of the continual progression of life throughout the year. It bestows a spirit of welcome to the visitor and indicates that the family is at home and looking forward to celebrating together.

Gold and silver glitter are rooted in tradition, for gold and silver were used only on special occasions. In some countries the tradition of using only real foliage for decoration is still clung to, while in many others, homes are decorated with artificial foliage or glittered boughs. Either way, the tradition of keeping Christmas decorations evergreen is carried on from year to year.

Blue candle (*above*) with silver foliage and sprigs of living holly on a cut section of wood. The dry foam can be glued to the wood.

Traditional red and gold (*above*) for an all-round design inserted into a block of polystyrene.

To make a door wreath (*above*), the material is bound to a metal hoop with thin wire.
Right: An unusual door wreath designed by a student at a German horticultural college and labelled as in the 'English style'. It is built on a wire base and tapered at each side. The material includes juniper, box, various artificial fruits and nuts, and red ribbon.

Gold silk roses and foliage in an onyx urn (*right*) are dressed for Christmas with the addition of fresh red carnations. The dried material is based in dry foam, so the living flowers must be put into water tubes prepared with wire 'legs' in the same way as for candles. Remember to fill with water each day. Many florists sell tubes, but if you cannot find any, impale a piece of soaked foam on top of the dry foam instead.

CHAPTER SIX

PERMANENT FLOWERS

Dried flowers and foliage – and many of the very beautiful
fabric flowers now available – can be great fun to arrange.
These arrangements are useful alternatives when fresh flowers
are not available from the garden, and a wonderful stand-by
for people who live in cities where fresh flowers can be
expensive in off-season periods.

Colourful arrangements made from last summer's flowers
and foliage can bring a note of nostalgia to long winter months
– just as the Victorians did when they kept dried flowers
between the pages of a favourite book to be reminded of a
special summer's day.

Included in this chapter are methods for preserving and
drying flowers, and how to make fabric flower designs for
display, head-dresses and posies.

DRIED FLOWER ARRANGEMENTS

In the winter months, when there are few fresh flowers to work with, dried flowers can provide particularly welcome decoration for the home. Large designs can fill empty fireplaces or the unused corners of rooms, and smaller arrangements can be made as centrepieces for occasional tables or mantlepieces. It is well worth putting time and trouble into your designs, since they will continue to look appealing for many months after you complete them.

With dried material, you can be very inventive in choosing containers since there is no problem of water seepage to consider. Pieces of driftwood, weathered wood and bark found on rambles might be employed, perhaps, or, for something more unusual, you could buy lengths of metal piping.

Dried flowers can also be used to decorate small boxes or wastepaper baskets, and they can make delightful pictures to hang on the wall. Miniatures can be really charming, but here it is important to choose material in the right proportion, and you will need tweezers to set the material in place. This may seem a slow exercise but it can be very satisfying to complete such a picture. Old frames, which can be cleaned and resprayed, are often to be found in salerooms. Instructions for making a large picture are given below.

There is always a vast and exciting choice of dried materials available from the florists, but if you grow your own flowers many of them can be dried very easily at home.

Some subjects dry more attractively than others. For example, if delphiniums are cut just before maturity, they will

The montbretia stems, moss and achillea head (*above*) are enhanced by this unusual handmade container.

Find a suitable base for the picture. Then assemble the bouquet. Secure the outline at the tying point, before gluing it to the base. Once the outline is in place, add the filling piece by piece.

eventually dry out keeping an almost perfect colour. They are best cut when about half the spikes show full colour. They should then be stood in about 2 in (5 cm) of water and allowed to condition thoroughly. Then hang them upside-down in a dry, draught-free place until they gradually dry out. A light coating with clear spray will help to keep the florets in place.

Achillea retains its golden colour for several years.

Helichrysums and statice are very popular as dried materials. They supply a wonderful variety of both colour and form. For people who grow their own helichrysums, remember to insert a wire through the flower head as soon as it is cut as, once it dries, it becomes almost too hard to pierce. Try to insert the wire up through a short stem so that it does not show. Then hang the flowers upside-down in small bunches ready for using in your winter arrangements.

Hydrangeas also keep their colour, particularly the green and red varieties, but the pale blue variety turns brown, although it is useful for masking the foam. It is best to strip the foliage from hydrangeas before leaving them to dry out.

Molucella bleaches to a delicate cream tint as it gradually dries. Arranged with grasses or fabric flowers, it makes very elegant line material and is long lasting.

Roses, also, can be dried on their natural stems, while almost any flower head can be quickly and successfully dried in silica gel. You need quite a large quantity, for the heads should be arranged in layers and copiously covered with the gel. This is available from most good chemist shops or from specialist suppliers of flower arranging materials.

This hollow log (*right*) is an ideal container for dried material. The base is covered to protect polished surfaces.

TYPES OF
FABRIC FLOWERS

Some people dislike the very thought of using imitation or permanent flowers and, certainly, there can be no substitute for the real thing, which is constantly changing, seasonal, exciting and sometimes unpredictable. Yet these flowers and plants that are made to imitate nature so exactly have a place in today's life-styles. They demand no conditioning, they will stay in place as they have been arranged and they will not wilt from lack of water.

Daffodils, daisies, ferns, gladioli, poppies and roses are all meticulously reproduced in a variety of sizes, colour, shapes and textures. In fact, there are very few flowers that are not now reproduced. There are also flowering plants, such as petunias, geraniums, hydrangeas and agapanthus, wisteria and laburnum, plus many other plants, which are correct in every detail and so convincing in appearance that one almost feels the need to water them.

Permanent flowers should be arranged with as much care as one gives to living material and the foam should be properly masked with either moss or foliage. In my view, bows of ribbon inserted into the centre of an arrangement do not make a substitute for careful masking. By all means add one or two bows if they enhance the general appearance of the arrangement. Be prepared to remove any unsightly stems and replace them with wire and tape. Some flowers, antirrhinums for example, are heavy and their stems will not support the flower head at the maximum stem-length. These have to be supplemented with extra wire or with slender canes attached with adhesive tape. This, of course, does not look very pretty, and should be used only if it can be hidden amongst the other flowers and foliage. The real thing has, of course,

1 To make a fabric flower arrangement, collect fabric flowers and foliage together in groups before preparing a container. Bright, mixed-coloured flowers have been chosen for this display.

2 First cut the correct size of brown floral foam and wedge it into the neck of a container and mask it with green moss.

3 Arrange the moss carefully so that moss and fabric foliage will appear very natural together.

4 Set the vertical and main lateral lines in position. The lateral material is set well back in the foam block to leave the front free.

strong enough stems to support the flower heads.

When buying permanent flowers and foliage, try to buy the best possible quality. These will withstand wind and weather, and having near permanent colours, will not fade in bright sunlight. They can also be washed providing you use very cool, soapy water (a detergent powder used sparingly is best). Rinse them carefully and lay them on a flat surface to dry naturally, then they will look as good as new.

5 Insert the remaining material in groups of similar colours to make the fullest use of a few flowers of each kind (*below*).

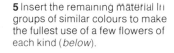

FABRIC FLOWER ARRANGEMENTS

Asymmetrical arrangement (*left*) in mixed flame colours.
Below: Cream anemones and café-au-lait coloured foliage arranged on a cork base.
Right: A spring design of daffodils, freesias and polyanthus in a dove-grey compote.

Some fabric flowers are so realistic it is almost impossible to tell them apart from fresh material. Many of the actual flowers are really lovely, but sometimes the stems, calyx and foliage are not quite in keeping, so it is necessary to strip the flower from the stem and re-wire and tape it. You may think it is far quicker to work with fabric material since it requires no conditioning, and it is more or less indestructible. In fact, some permanent flowers need a surprising amount of preparation. However, the time spent is not wasted because your arrangement will last for just as long as you want it to.

Some fabric flowers are purely decorative and do not faithfully resemble any living material; they are useful simply from the point of view of colour, shape and size. Then there are those that are blatantly imitation but that are still very decorative and fun to use. For example,

huge gold and silver open roses, which, if used in the right place at the right time, are really effective. They can be used for gold or silver anniversaries, at Christmas or birthday parties or to decorate a special gift-wrapped parcel.

Fabric flower and foliage arrangements should be based in Oasis-sec or a similar product; ordinary foam used dry is not nearly firm enough and may easily break apart. Drihard is another product

that gives an extremely firm base, but being a type of cement it dries not only very hard but very fast. Thus one needs to work with both speed and precision since there is rarely a chance to change your mind once a stem has been placed.

Both foam base and Drihard should be masked, either with grey reindeer moss or ordinary green moss, both of which should be soaked in clean water to make them supple. The moss can then be

pinned to the base with small wire hairpins; it quickly dries, retaining its original colour.

Choose whichever moss blends better with the flowers; for example, spring flowers, daffodils, freesias and polyanthus would look more realistic based with green moss, while most dried material and the pale browns and creams of some fabric flowers look better with the reindeer moss.

FABRIC BOUQUET
AND HAT

Fabric flowers can be used to make a bouquet or for the head-dresses of a bride and her bridesmaids. The bride's mother might also trim her wedding hat with a design of silk flowers, perhaps, or make a handsome corsage for her outfit. On a more casual level, a single fabric poppy can cheer the most battered straw boater. The possibilities are seemingly endless.

Fabric flowers and foliage, while easier to handle than real flowers, need almost as much preparation as living material. Each flower has to be wired and taped, and the finished result should be at least as delicate as a real flower design. Carefully worked, however, a fabric flower design might last you a lifetime.

This charming bride's head-dress (*below*) is made in soft pinks to match the bouquet opposite. The flowers are wired and taped individually, and the finished arrangement is held on with hair grips (bobby pins) hidden underneath the foliage.

1 To make a fabric bouquet, the flowers and leaves are first wired and taped separately. The material is then arranged and secured at a central point and bound very tightly with fine wire. Final adjustments can be made to the positions of the flowers and leaves.

2 From the back, all lines should be seen to radiate from one central point.
3 The finished fabric bouquet (*right*). The handle has been bound with ribbon to make it more comfortable to hold.